WHO ARE THE SCOTS?

WHO ARE THE SCOTS?

Edited by Gordon Menzies

BRITISH BROADCASTING CORPORATION

Acknowledgment is due to the following for permission to reproduce illustrations:

BANFF MUSEUM (photo: National Museum of Antiquities) Celtic trumpet, Deskford (Plate 3); DEPARTMENT OF AERIAL PHOTOGRAPHY, UNIVERSITY OF CAMBRIDGE Mote of Urr (Plate 12); HUNTERIAN MUSEUM, GLASGOW Roman distance slab, Hutcheson Hill (Plate 4); TOM WEIR Iona Abbey (and St Martin's Cross) (Plate 7); DEPARTMENT OF THE ENVIRONMENT (Crown copyright) Ring of Brodgar (Plate 1); Broch of Mousa (Plate 2); Pictish symbol stone, Glamis Manse (Plate 5); Pictish symbol stone, Aberlemno Churchyard (Plate 5); Dumbarton Rock (Plate 6); Ruthwell Cross (Plate 9); Anglian panel, Jedburgh Abbey (Plate 11); Norse settlement, Jarlshof, Shetland (Plate 13); Norman church, Leuchars (Plate 15); Dirleton Castle (Plate 16); Pictish symbol stone (Cover); NATIONAL MUSEUM OF ANTIQUITIES, EDINBURGH Monymusk Reliquary (Plate 8); Kildalton Cross (Plate 10); Skaill Hoard, Orkney (Plate 14); THAMES AND HUDSON LTD. Pictish symbols from *The Picts* by Isabel Henderson

Acknowledgement is also due to Alan Small, University of Dundee, for permission to reproduce *Norse longhouse in Unst* (Figure 14).

The maps and drawings are by David Brown

First published 1971 Reprinted 1971, 1975

Published by the British Broadcasting Corporation
35 Marylebone High Street, London WIM 4AA
Printed in England by Tonbridge Printers Ltd., Tonbridge, Kent
ISBN: 0 563 10597 6

Contents

Illustrations

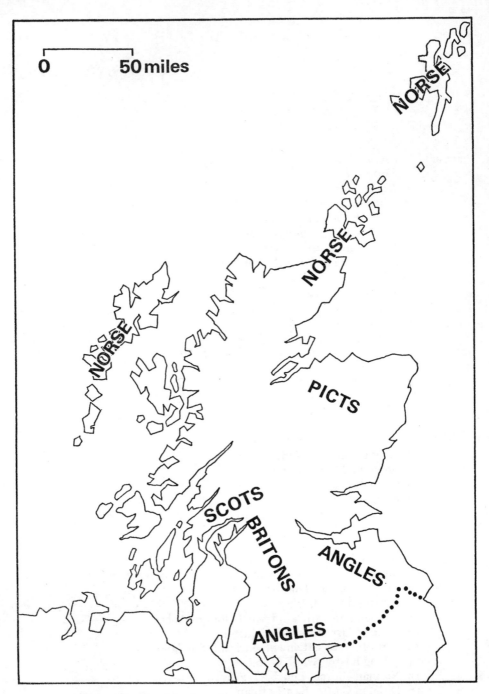

Fig 1   Scotland in the 9th century A.D.

Foreword

'Who are the Scots?' is the title of a television series produced by BBC Scotland's educational broadcasting department. As producer of the television series I conceived it as an archaeological/historical investigation into the sources of the Scottish nation. But television by its very nature tends to be ephemeral and it seemed logical to have a book to complement the series and to provide more permanent material for those interested in the beginnings and the shaping of Scotland. There is an increasing interest in the past, an awareness of a distinctive Scottish heritage and culture, and, perhaps, a deeply-felt need for some kind of identity in the wider world of today.

In terms of archaeology and history this is a good time for re-assessment and re-appraisal. The bulldozer, that symbol of progress, is gradually obliterating the evidence of history. More and more people are being persuaded that positive steps must be taken to preserve certain aspects of their heritage. Modern scientific technique is not necessarily the enemy of archaeology and, indeed, in some respects it has become an invaluable ally. Pollen analysis, dating by radiocarbon sampling of organic material from archaeological sites and thermo-luminescence dating of pottery and other artefacts, are providing the archaeologist with much more accurate information on prehistoric peoples and their relationships with each other.

Our story begins with the hunters and gatherers who found their way north in the fifth millennium B.C. and we take it right up to the thirteenth century A.D. Many people came to Scotland during these six thousand years. But who are the Scots? Are they to be found among our prehistoric ancestors who clung to the sea-shore, or among the Beaker people who came from Holland and the Rhineland, or among that other continental group, the iron-using Celts who resisted the Romans from their hill-forts? Are the Scots, perhaps, more genuinely to be found among the enigmatic Picts, or the Irish Scots of Dalriada, or among their contemporaries, the British tribes who survived the Roman occupation, the Angles of Northumbria and latterly, the vigorous Norsemen who began to colonise the north and west around A.D. 800? Who, then, was a Scot in that turbulent ninth century? And later still, in the eleventh and twelfth centuries, yet another ingredient was thrown into the melting-pot of the Scottish nation – the Anglo-Normans, whose ultimate contributions were stability and organised government.

Perhaps some of the regional differences of present-day Scotland find their roots in our history. Could it be that the distinctive character of the folk of the north-east has something to do with the fact that Aberdeenshire, Kincardineshire and Angus was pre-eminently the area of the Picts? Obviously that somewhat mysterious quality associated with the Gaelic-speaking islander reflects the earlier Christian culture of the Scots of Dalriada. And perhaps the hard-headed Lowlander, that canny Scot of history, owes much to the influence of the Angles and Normans.

Many people have contributed to the preparation of this book and I am deeply grateful to all those in universities, museums and the BBC itself who so generously provided help, guidance and advice. I particularly would like to thank Kenneth Jackson, Professor of Celtic Studies in the University of Edinburgh, for his valuable suggestions on the controversial Dark Age period of Scotland's history. I have conceived my task as editor of this book as one of streamlining the various contributions, of reaching common ground in terminology and spelling, and of avoiding obvious overlaps between the chapters. I have not attempted to resolve opposing views or apparent contradictions. Archaeology and history, as we all know, are a matter of interpretation, and differences of opinion must surely bring the past to life.

Many new peoples came to Scotland in the six thousand years of our story but change must have been painfully slow and changes must have been even more painfully achieved. There were invasions, conquests, perhaps exterminations, more often assimilations. But certainly by the time of Wallace and Bruce a recognisable entity called Scotland was in being. Whatever may have happened to Scotland since the thirteenth century, and certainly thousands of people have come and gone in recent centuries, there is no gainsaying the fact that the nation we know as Scotland and the people called 'Scots' had come into being by 1296. And that is where this story ends – with the threat of English domination facing the Scottish people. In such a crisis a nation found itself.

GORDON MENZIES

CHAPTER I

The First Peoples

Stuart Piggott

Something over six thousand years ago the indigenous population
of large mammals in Scotland received the addition of a new exotic
species, that wily predator Man. For millennia large tracts of
northern Europe had been uninhabitable, buried beneath the vast
ice-sheets of the glacial periods, and when, from ten thousand
or more years ago, these began their final northward retreat as the
result of slow but decisive climatic changes that were moving towards modern conditions, it was long before that rare animal, Man,
colonised north Britain. With the changing climate came changes
in plant cover, as tundra and taiga gave way to forests of birch
and pine, and these in turn to deciduous woodlands dominated by
oak. Wherever forests could establish themselves they encroached
and flourished, inhibited only by salt marshes or altitude, or by
residual adverse climatic conditions in northerly latitudes and
wind-swept islands. The background against which we must set the
first human population of Scotland, as elsewhere in northern
Europe, is one dominated by vegetation, to which all animals were
adapted, and existed in reciprocal relationship to natural stands of
timber or open grass-land; to moors or to hill pasture; to marsh or
sand-dunes. It was man alone who, as a part of his specific
peculiarities, became increasingly over the centuries not only
another mammal adapting himself to his living environment of
fellow-beasts and plants, but a conscious agent in modifying his
surroundings and exploiting them deliberately to his own ends.

By around 6000 B.C. the changes in land and sea level resulting
from the release of pressure from the retreating ice-sheets and the
increase in water following on their partial melting, had among
other changes caused a northern European promontory to become
the present islands of Britain and Ireland with the formation of
the English Channel. In the southern part of this original land-
mass a tiny human population had formed the most north-westerly
area of habitation, on the edge of the European world of early
mankind, from immensely early times, and now, with the formation
of the Channel, this island population was probably to be reckoned

in terms of a few hundred persons living the lives of hunters and gatherers with stone as their only material for edge-tools, in common with their relatives in what was now the western European land-mass.

As the climate slowly ameliorated, and forests spread over what had been the open tundra south of the ice-sheet, the reindeer, which had been the main meat supply of the early hunters, migrated northward with their shifting natural habitat, and woodland species such as red deer and elk took their place. Man, adaptive after a couple of million years not only of genetic evolution but of the social transmitted skills that distinguished him from other animals, remained in possession of the new landscape and changed his ways to ensure his continued survival in novel circumstances. The archaeological changes in his tool-kit reflect this adaptation to change, and with forest growth the relatively open sea-coasts provided good settlement areas for those who could turn to the harvest of the sea for their source of protein. It is with such stone-using hunters and fishers that the story of man in Scotland begins.

Remains of camp-sites, archaeologically represented by tools of stone, bone and antler, charcoal from fires, or the piles of shells from edible molluscs, have been found in Scotland from the Tweed Valley to the Forth, and up the east coast, or again in the west on the coasts and islands. Radiocarbon dating now gives a minimum time-span from before 4000 B.C. to 3500 and probably to 3000 B.C. for such sites, and we have to reckon once again with a population comparable with recent hunting-gathering groups such as the Caribou Eskimos, of about a dozen persons to 100 square miles. It has been reasonably estimated that the total population of Britain at this time need not have exceeded eight or nine thousand persons, living in small hunting bands of 15 or 20 individuals, and coming nowhere near to exploiting the full food capacity afforded by the red deer population alone, let alone other resources. Wild cattle were another woodland species, as were boars, and wild horses seem to have existed in Caithness at least : brown bears and beavers were also among the Scottish fauna. On the coasts stranded whales and seals were certainly hacked into for meat and blubber – Rorqual and Blue Whales in the Firth of Forth, and Grey and Spotted Seals in Oronsay, have been found with evidence of human exploitation at this time. This coastal activity, and the colonisation of islands, shows that boats were in use, probably skin-covered in the manner of the Eskimo *umiak* or the ancestor of the Irish curragh, and it is hardly surprising that fish that can only be caught by off-shore fishing from a boat, such as wrasse or sea-bream, conger and ray, were being eaten by the island fishermen in the west.

The boat, which as we see must have been in use at this time, is a notable addition to human technology. The Scottish west coast communities were very probably in touch with, and may even have been derived from, similar peoples in Western France; the type of mattock with a shaft-hole used by them and by the whale-eaters in the Forth is in common with those of the contemporary hunter-fisher groups of Denmark and North Germany. Once Britain was an island, outside contacts would only be maintained by sea, and the introduction of new peoples and ideas henceforward depended on boats and boatmen, as did the movements of population not only along the rivers and coasts, offering easier going than land travel through forest and swamp, but the colonisation of islands such as the Hebrides, Orkney and Shetland. Here was a decisive and conscious extension of human capabilities, whereby man made himself amphibious without the necessity of even getting wet.

Opinion is more and more tending, as the result of new investigations by archaeologists and botanists, in the direction of seeing these early hunting peoples in Britain as actual agents in the first attack on the forest cover by deliberate and selective burning, presumably to increase opportunities for hunting, in the manner of the North American Indians in recent times, or otherwise making clearances. It is of course impossible to rule out accidental fires caused by lightning rather than humans, but at Benn Eighe in Wester Ross layers of charcoal in the peat at early dates might well be due to human agencies, and similarly the reduction of forest hinted at in the pollen sequences at Loch Creag near Aberfeldy, Netherly Moss in Kincardineshire, and in the Grampians, at a date around 5000 B.C., could again be due to the earliest human communities in Scotland rather than unidentified natural processes.

For hunters and gatherers, occasional and sporadic inroads on the natural forest cover may from time to time be advantageous, but are not a necessity in maintaining subsistence. When, however, we consider economies based on mixed farming, with stock demanding grazing, and cereal crops necessitating cleared sunlit areas of land, we find man actively engaged in modifying the landscape as a condition of survival. The development of such economies in antiquity must have come about by almost imperceptible shifts in emphasis in the relationship of man as an animal to his fellow-beasts and to the vegetable world within which he and they had their being. In the Old World the archaeological evidence for the earliest tentative changes in subsistence-economy from hunting and gathering to a control of certain animals and plants for exploitation as food resources is on present showing in restricted areas of the Near East, but the problem now goes far beyond the old simplicities of a 'Neolithic Revolution' in one spot. For our present purpose we need pursue this matter of remote origins no further, since the first agriculture in Scotland, as elsewhere in the British Isles, is the result of the direct importation of new economies by actual colonists from continental Europe, bringing with them not only ideas, but the stock and seed whereby to put them into practice. But we must look rather more closely at the situation in Europe from around 3500 B.C., for it is not long after this date that we can trace the first appearance all over the British Isles of the new colonies of stone-using agriculturalists, growing cereal crops and with four or five domestic species of animals, making pottery, and building permanent settlements, ceremonial monuments and grandiose tombs. In the old archaeological terminology, this is Neolithic culture, impinging upon and soon superseding the earlier Mesolithic hunting and gathering economy. It was to set the agrarian norm for pre-industrial Britain, modified over the millennia only by technological increments first of copper and bronze working, and later iron, and when the improving landlords in Scotland in the middle of the eighteenth century A.D. sought to replace an archaic and ineffective system with modern techniques, they were bringing to an end the decrepit and effete descendant of an agriculture which was probably far more efficient in the eighteenth century B.C.

Earlier concepts of the course of colonisation in prehistoric Britain tended to the simplistic view of one or two south-coast landings, followed by an inexorable and slow spread of population northwards over many centuries. But the numerous radiocarbon dates from England, Wales and Ireland, together with the half-dozen we have from Scotland, all go to show that settlements of the new agriculturalists, or the disturbances in pollen frequencies likely to be due to forest clearance, were taking place almost everywhere in the British Isles within a century or so on either side of 3000 B.C. in radiocarbon terms, and probably more like 4500 B.C.

in calendar years. (Probably owing to cosmic changes, e.g. solar radiation, radiocarbon years diverge from calendar years, but the subject is still under discussion.) A stone-chambered tomb in Arran seems first to have been used about 3160 B.C., and the timber mortuary house within a round barrow at Pitnacree near Aberfeldy around 2860 B.C. We have so far no other early dates in Scotland, but settlements in Bute and at Grandtully in Perthshire were both inhabited about 2120 B.C. We have in fact the repetition of the general British pattern of chronology, with dates covering rather over a millennium from before 3000 to around 2000 B.C. in radiocarbon years, but probably to be spread over twice this span (4500 – 2500 B.C.) in true time. At all events, we must think of a very long period of time within which to place our first stone-using agriculturalists and their surviving monuments. Even on the short time-scale the total of a thousand or so stone-chambered monumental tombs in Scotland need not represent an excessive demand on the labour resources of however small a population when building could theoretically be distributed over as many years.

Demographic figures for populations comparable with our first agriculturalists are far more difficult to estimate than the hunter-gatherers, whose economy has survived to recent times. We can only assume an initial colonising nucleus interbreeding with the indigenous population, and a subsequent exponential growth. If our earlier figures are multiplied by 10, we would have a population of 1.2 persons to the square mile; by 20, 2.4, and so on. It is impossible even to make a reasoned guess, but one may compare the estimated figures for the Domesday Book population of late eleventh century England, about 26 persons to the square mile, or that of pre-industrial Scotland in the 1801 census of 56 to the square mile: the estimated 2 million inhabitants of Roman Britain would give a density around that of the Domesday Book figure. Such comparisons at least give a rough scale, and the likelihood throughout prehistory is of a population incredibly small by our modern standards, but with the construction of the numerous monuments which indicate its existence today spread out over an extremely long period of time.

The wild ancestors of the staple crops of wheat and barley are grasses growing in natural conditions in the Near East and perhaps eastern Europe. As farming communities pushed north-westwards into the central European forests and beyond, they were taking what were by now cultivated cereals further and further away from their natural environment, and as an inevitable result, the more resistant strains survived. By what we have seen is a minimal date around 3500 B.C., stone-using agricultural communities – the later Neolithic cultures of archaeology – were established on the Continent up to the shores of the Atlantic, the Channel and the North Sea. Wheat and barley, the former preponderating, were grown, and, also of south-eastern ancestry, domestic sheep and goats, cattle and pigs, were being bred. The dog had been domesticated by the northern hunter-gatherers, but new breeds were also introduced. Cattle formed the most important item of stock for most communities. By shortly before 3000 B.C. the colonisation of the British Isles was beginning, however few in numbers the Founding Fathers, with contributions probably from the whole north-western European seaboard from Biscay to the Baltic. This was the phase of innovation, to be followed by consolidation and the development of insular and distinctive qualities.

Agriculture was already partly, if not wholly, with the ox-drawn plough rather than hoe or digging-stick : actual traces of ploughed field surfaces have been recovered in south England with dates before 2700 B.C. and in Shetland are surviving surface traces of the farm steadings of stone-using agriculturalists of probably a millennium later but conserving earlier traditions, with houses, field walls and clearance-heaps of stones. One of these, on the Scord of Brouster, has five or six irregularly defined fields totalling $2\frac{3}{4}$ acres (about 1 ha), comparable to a modern Shetland croft; evidence of ploughing is provided by stone 'bar-shares' with worn tips found also in Orkney. The Shetland crop was barley, a cache of 28 lb. (nearly 13 kg.) of burnt grain being found in a contemporary house of the standard local oval form with massive stone and turf walls, with a thatched roof carried on internal wood posts.

In Orkney the shortage of timber at a date probably around 2000 B.C. led to the construction of remarkable settlements in which not only houses, but their internal fittings such as beds and sets of shelves, were built wholly of stone, and so have survived. Skara Brae is the most famous of these sites : here although animals were domesticated, there is no evidence of agriculture. Cattle predominated, of a distinctive breed, with evidence for castration, and the predominance of young animals in the food debris was taken to imply regular autumn slaughter, in contrast to the sheep, almost as important in the Skara Brae economy as cattle, which seem to have been over-wintered. Some red deer were hunted, and fishing was carried out from boats.

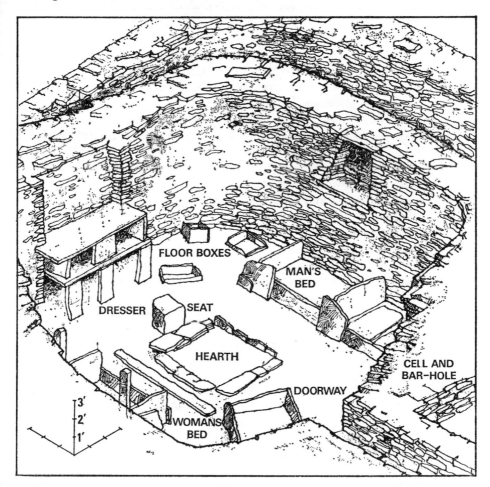

Fig 2   Skara Brae house interior

The basic individual plan within the agglomeration of thick-walled structures embedded deep in circumjacent midden material was a square room with rounded corners, with stone-framed bed-boxes to right and left of the entrance, that on the right averaging 6 ft. 6 in. (2 m.) in length as against 5 ft. 2 in. (1.6 m.) on the left, and so presumably for man and wife. There was a central square hearth, burning peat, and at the similar site of Rinyo on Rousay were remains of small square clay-built ovens. Opposite the door was a 'dresser' of stone shelves and uprights, and clay-luted 'boxes' in the floor could have held water (and indeed live fish or lobsters!) The roof was probably carried on rafters of drift-wood or whale's bones. Such a house-type is a well-contrived adaptation to adverse weather conditions and it is hardly surprising that substantially the same plan was used up until recent times among the Eskimoes.

We have seen how the first agricultural colonisation of Britain presupposes adequate boats, and subsequent coastal and inter-island traffic must have been continuous, as would have been the use of rivers and lochs. So far as land transport is concerned, castrated cattle could imply ox traction not only for ploughs but for vehicles such as sledges and slide-cars, or even wheeled carts and wagons. Block-wheeled vehicles were in use among stone-using agricultura-lists at least in Holland and Denmark well before 2000 B.C., but evidence from Britain is at present lacking. However communica-tions were established, there is no doubt that these early com-munities, while to a large degree self-sufficient, were nevertheless not completely isolated entities.

The necessity of obtaining adequate stone for flaking or grinding into various tools led early on to the selection and transportation of suitable rocks up to many miles from their source and in Scotland it appears that the hunter-gatherers of the fourth millennium B.C. had at least a localised west coast 'trade' in Rhum bloodstone, and Arran pitchstone reached sites as far east as Fife and the Tweed Valley. With the need for tough stone for axe-blades the first agriculturalists not only sought material widely, but soon after the initial colonisation of the British Isles organised centres of manu-facture from particularly suitable rocks in Cornwall, North Wales, the Lake District and Northern Ireland, concurrently with mining and producing flint axes in the south English chalk areas. Scotland not only participated in the ensuing trade, but at Creag na Caillich near Killin developed a working-site that can hardly be unique. The detection of this trade depends upon the collaboration of archaeologists and petrologists, and depends on numerous precise microscopic identifications, but the volume of trade in axes from the Antrim workshops is already apparent, extending to Aberdeenshire in some bulk and reaching even Lewis and Shetland. So too axes from Great Langdale in the Lake District, and from Graig Lwyd in North Wales, were in use in the third millennium Scotland. One very remarkable group of what can only be ceremonial axe-blades of jade have an as yet unknown Continental source, possibly in Switzerland, and here the two dozen specimens from Scotland represent participation in an international phenomenon.

We know less of the exploitation of flint in Scotland, where there are no natural sources of good quality, and, except for the sites of Skelmuir and Boddam in north-east Scotland, apparently quarried in prehistoric times, beach pebbles would alone provide material. Some seems to have been imported, probably from Yorkshire and Antrim. Research in southern England has demonstrated a trade in pottery from the early third millennium, and this cannot have been a circumstance unique in Britain. In one way and another, there must have been a brisk coming and going within the British Isles and across to the Continent, foreshadowing the contacts to be developed in the second millennium when copper, tin and gold had become necessary items in the basic economy.

But man's needs transcend subsistence-economics, and indeed it is only we sophisticates who isolate these from the world of the irrational, and separate secular from sacred. The jade axe-blades hint at a world of lost ceremonials, the exchange of gifts pleasing to men and the gods alike, and the most enduring memorials to our first farming forebears in Scotland are their monumental tombs and their ceremonial centres. Something more than a thousand burial places to be dated roughly between the minimum dates of 3000 – 2000 B.C. survive north of the Border, architecturally re-lated to others in England, Wales and Ireland as clearly as one medieval church to another – indeed like the churches of the Christian Middle Ages, their counterparts have an ecumenical distribution in Europe, and reflect the variations in burial practice, and so by inference religious custom and belief, within the com-munities of the third millennium European north-west.

Before 3000 B.C. in southern England structures for the collective burial of groups of individuals were being made, embodying elaborate and sometimes huge enclosures and mortuary houses of hewn timber, eventually covered with great elongated mounds of earth and rubble. Architecturally, these long barrows have similarities with contemporary monuments on the north European plain that can scarcely be coincidental, and practically as early, they were being built as far north as Yorkshire. Their rare representatives are now being identified and excavated in southern and eastern Scotland, as at Lochhill, Kirkcudbrightshire and Dalladies, Kincardineshire, the former with a timber mortuary house of a type also represented in Scotland under a round barrow at Pitnacree, near Aberfeldy. In Scotland too, as in England, long cairns may be associated with stone-built burial chambers, and in the north the question may be complicated by a stone-chambered tomb in a round cairn being later incorporated in an elongated structure. We must turn to the type of monumental tomb with stone chamber and approach-passage under a circular cairn before going further into these complications.

Such tombs have a very wide west European distribution, from Iberia to Brittany and from Wales and Ireland to north Scotland, Orkney and Shetland, and were at one time thought to represent some form of colonisation or missionary movement from the southwest, and indeed the Mediterranean. Now, while the architectural similarities remain demonstrable, radiocarbon dating and other factors make this idea impossible to sustain in simplified form, though there must have been coming and going between local groups of tomb-builders. In Scotland, Maes Howe in Orkney represents perhaps the highest point of architectural skill in such monuments in northern Europe, certainly in Britain, and other less magnificent tombs of this type are widespread in the west and north. Other chambered tombs represent either the tradition of the long cairn with terminal chamber from the start, or, as we said, hybrid monuments embodying more than one architectural tradition, and the tombs of the Clyde and Solway estuaries show both forms. In all, we are dealing with formally expressed architectural solutions to problems posed by the requirements of funeral rituals now irrevocably lost, and not only a set of technical building skills, but a command and organisation of labour beyond that possible to the members of an ordinary family. Behind the great chambered tombs we glimpse authority, and circumstances in which this authority can express itself in works of communal effort. These implications again lie behind other ceremonial sites, not primarily for funeral purposes.

Here again we are dealing with a phenomenon spread over the British Isles, though hardly in Europe. Enclosed areas, with circular banks and ditches, upright timbers (or timber buildings), standing stones, or pits inexplicable except as ritual, are widely distributed in Britain, and their building in southern England at least, where we have radiocarbon dates, goes back to the first farming communities in the middle third millennium B.C. Their sanctity, and indeed their building, continued well into the second millennium, and imparts an element of continuity not present in the burial custom, which changes from collective to single-grave burial as a result of newcomers from the Continent on the eve of the technological change to bronze-working.

On Cairnpapple Hill in West Lothian such a sanctuary began somewhere before 2000 B.C. with a setting of ritual pits, soon succeeded by an embanked enclosure containing an oval of standing stones. This in turn was dismantled and the stones re-used in a tomb of about 1500 B.C., later itself remodelled and further burials added. Here continuity is demonstrable by excavation, but other ceremonial centres, such as the Ring of Brodgar in Orkney, became the focus of subsequent veneration, round which were set the burial mounds of the later faithful. It is this continuity in prehistory, with the internal development of societies no less than the adoption of new ideas or technologies from outside, that make the old archaeological scheme of 'Ages' of Stone, Bronze and Iron outmoded and even obstructive today. When we move in subsequent chapters to the interplay of innovation and tradition in later prehistory, and thence into history, we shall see repeated familiar patterns of change and assimilation, but behind all lie the basic agricultural economies developed by 3000 B.C. and introduced to Scotland in the circumstances sketched above.

CHAPTER II

Metal Workers

Graham and Anna Ritchie

Most archaeological evidence datable to the second millennium B.C. is provided by burial or ritual structures and by the artefacts or grave-goods associated with them. Little is known about the domestic life of the period, apart from a few settlements such as Skara Brae and Rinyo in Orkney, Stanydale in Shetland and Northton in Harris. These have survived because they were built of stone and also because they were buried beneath sand-blows. Grave-goods provide a very partial record of life in the second millennium B.C., and, as they were specially chosen to accompany the dead, they are not necessarily typical of everyday domestic utensils. This is particularly true of pottery, some of which appears to have been made specifically for burial purposes.

The first few centuries of the second millennium saw the arrival of small groups of people from the continent, characterised by a distinct type of pottery vessel, known as a 'Beaker', and by a new burial tradition. In contrast to the collective or multiple burial rite of the neolithic farmers, the makers of Beaker pottery favoured individual interments in small stone coffins or 'cists'. From a study of their skeletal remains, it is clear that these new settlers belonged to a physical type distinct from that represented in chambered cairns; they were rather taller than the original population, with a broader face and shorter skull. They represent the third strand in the make-up of the prehistoric population of Scotland, following the hunters and farmers described in the first chapter.

Some of the earliest types of Beaker have been found on the east coast of Scotland, particularly among the sand dunes of Fife and East Lothian, a distribution that reflects the route of their makers across the North Sea. There are also early examples in western Scotland at Glenluce in Wigtownshire and in Ardnamurchan. The decorative motifs on these early Beakers include horizontal rows of impressions made by a twisted cord, and linear designs executed with a toothed comb; analogies for this decoration can be found in the Low Countries, and it is thought that the settlers who reached Scotland soon after 2,000 B.C. originated from that area. There is little evidence of hostile intent on the part of these new arrivals, although barbed-and-tanged flint arrowheads indicate the use of the bow, and a few copper or bronze objects show that even these earliest Beaker groups possessed some knowledge of metal-working.

A second and more complex series of intrusions has been dated to about the eighteenth century B.C., when the coastal plain of eastern Scotland from the Tweed to the Moray Firth was settled by more Beaker-using people from Holland and the Rhineland. The pottery decoration, initially akin to styles current on the continent, developed local traits and motifs over the following few centuries. This pottery is associated with barbed-and-tanged arrowheads, archers' wrist-guards, flint knives and scrapers, jet beads of various forms and a small number of copper or bronze objects. A local metal industry was gradually established, as well as trade links with the sources of ore.

In several cases, Beakers have been found either among the grave-goods in a chambered tomb or in the material blocking access to the tomb; this suggests that the change in burial custom from collective to individual graves took place gradually. The newcomers built round cairns or barrows covering their burials in contrast to the elongated mounds of the earlier period, but this change in the form of surviving field-monuments does not imply that the overall pattern of life was much altered.

The site of Cairnpapple (West Lothian) and the cairns in the Kilmartin area of Mid-Argyll provide useful series to illustrate the changes in burial and ritual activity during the second millennium B.C. At the same time, they show the continuing sanctity of certain areas or indeed of individual sites. Four phases of the Cairnpapple sequence belong to the period following 2000 B.C., the earliest being a setting of upright stones (represented only by the holes in which they had been placed) and a series of deposits of cremated bone in pits. This is a sanctuary and burial site of pre-Beaker farmers, and must date to around 2000 B.C. A much more elaborate ritual site is of Beaker date (1700–1600 B.C.), when the earlier stones were removed. The Beaker sanctuary or temple, for such it must have been, consisted of an oval enclosure, or henge monument; this comprised a bank with internal ditch through which there were entrances at the north and south ends. Just within this earthwork there was an oval setting of standing stones. Rather off-centre, but beside the setting of the first period, there was a grave-pit which contained two Beaker pots and traces of a wooden club. This burial was probably covered by a small kerbed cairn and there was an impressive standing stone at the head of the grave. A second Beaker burial was discovered near one of the stones of the oval 'circle'. This vessel has affinities with those found in the North Rhineland, while the two in the grave belong to a more local style.

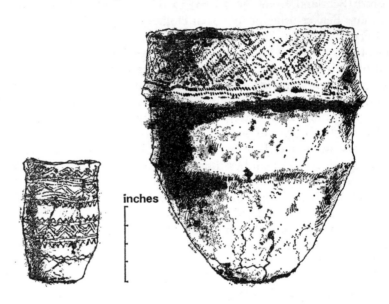

inches

Fig 3 Beaker (Cairnpapple); Cinerary Urn (Cairnpapple)

Henge monuments are unknown among Beaker communities on the Continent, but, as has already been shown, single-entrance henges have been found in late neolithic contexts in Britain. This phase at Cairnpapple shows that there was a fusing of intrusive elements (the individual grave with its covering cairn) with native ideas (the sacred situation and the henge type of monument). Given this amalgam of traditions, it is hardly surprising that a pottery type owing much to the earlier neolithic wares should have evolved; although the origin of this Food Vessel style is still under discussion, it is clearly an insular phenomenon. In the third period of Cairnpapple (1500 B.C.), the stone circle was taken down and some of the stones were used as the kerb of a large cairn about 50 ft. in diameter. Its central cist contained a Food Vessel, which had accompanied an inhumation burial, and a stone bearing three cup-markings. This mound completely enveloped the earlier Beaker grave. Both the Food Vessel cist and Beaker grave may be seen within the hollow concrete mound which has been built to simulate this cairn. In the fourth period (1400 B.C.), the cairn was doubled in size and two cremation burials within Cinerary Urns were inserted. This pottery style is also of insular origin, and, with the predominance of cremation burial, the influence of the foreign elements represented initially by Beaker pottery came to an end.

A fascinating series of sites at Kilmartin, Mid Argyll, provides another microcosm of burial monuments of the first half of the second millennium B.C. Here the sites are disposed in a straight line extending in either direction from a chambered cairn, Nether Largie South. In this tomb there was a primary deposit of neolithic ware and a secondary series of burials accompanied by Beaker pottery. One of two secondary cists within the cairn material contained a Food Vessel burial. There are three other cairns to the north and one to the south of this cairn, and it is likely that these were added one after the other deliberately to form a linear cemetery. The cairns of Nether Largie Centre and North contained cists without accompanying grave-goods, but the cover slab and one end-slab from the latter cairn are remarkable for their decoration; a series of cup-marks and representations of flat axes have been pecked into the surfaces of the slabs. Further to the north, the Glebe Cairn covered two large cists with pottery of Food Vessel type.

Other ceremonial or religious sites which date to the first half of the second millennium are standing stones and stone circles, and the purpose of these enigmatic monuments has long puzzled archaeologists. Some stone circles certainly contained burials, but it has recently been suggested that the setting of stones has an astronomical significance. This cannot at present be proved, but the lay-out of stones to form ellipses and flattened circles, as well as true circles, demonstrates the mathematical precision with which they were designed.

During the second half of the second millennium B.C. and contemporary with burials accompanied by Cinerary Urns, a flourishing trade in metal-work existed in Scotland. With the exception of razors, awls and small blades, these bronze objects have not been found as grave-goods, possibly because the metal was too valuable to lose in that way. The range of bronze types includes tools such as axes, chisels and knife-blades, weapons such as spearheads, dirks and rapiers, and a few examples of personal ornaments such as torcs. Most of the surviving ornaments were made of gold. A few of the stone moulds have been discovered in which spearheads and axes had been cast, and two anvils, a hammerhead and four punches have survived as evidence of the metal-worker's tool kit. The anvils and the hammerhead were found in Sutherland and Nairn, and it has been suggested that this may indicate that trade in beaten metalwork did not extend to the far north, thus encouraging production by local craftsmen. All the tools and weapons were apparently designed to take wooden handles or shafts, although the wood has not survived; in the case of spearheads, a socket was cast into which the shaft would be rammed, and there were in some cases holes or loops by which a cord might provide additional fastening to the shaft. The production of socketed axes was not established until the eighth century B.C., probably because the type was difficult to cast before the introduction of lead into the bronze alloy (thus improving its casting quality). During the earlier period, axes were made with flanges which clasped the wooden haft, the whole being bound with cord to strengthen it. Razors and knives had tangs which would be inserted into the handles, and the hilts of dirks and rapiers were riveted into position.

One of the most significant innovations among bronze artefacts early in the first millennium B.C. is the sword, for it implies a change in fighting tactics from stabbing to slashing. The ten or eleven Scottish examples of beaten bronze shields have been assigned to the eighth century B.C.

Considerable contact with areas outside Scotland is apparent among the bronze objects, belonging to the early centuries of the first millennium B.C.; there was strong contact with Ireland and southern England, areas with which Scotland shared ideas in metalworking derived ultimately from northern Europe. Foreign contacts were intensified by the seventh century B.C., when two classes of objects in particular point to trade relations with the continental Celts; these are beaten bronze vessels, horse-harness and cart fittings. The buckets, thought to have contained wine, and the cauldrons were swiftly copied by native craftsmen with Scottish examples dating from the later eighth century and earlier seventh century B.C. Horse-harness and the fittings of a miniature cult-wagon found in a hoard at Horsehope (Peeblesshire) indicate that the domesticated horse and the wheeled vehicle were known, and possibly in use, by the end of the seventh century B.C., at least in south-east Scotland.

The houses of a small community belonging to a period within the seventh to sixth centuries B.C. have survived at Jarlshof on the promontory of Sumburgh Head in Shetland. Traces of an enclosing wall across the promontory remain, but the nature of the site was essentially non-defensive; the houses are stone-built in the existing prehistoric Shetland tradition, with thick walls and internal bays or compartments. The activities of a bronze-smith are represented among the artefacts by broken fragments of clay moulds for casting bronze swords, socketed axes and ornamental pins, and it is these moulds that provide dating evidence for the site. The inhabitants used pottery and tools of bone and stone, kept oxen and were partial, in their diet, to limpets. Grain was milled in stone querns of trough-type, and, although the presence of querns need not imply that cereals were cultivated on the spot, traces of small corn-plots may be attributable to this phase. Stone bar-shares for use on the simple plough known as the bow ard have been found in contexts at least as early as the second millennium B.C. in Shetland.

It is an unfortunate fact that few bronze artefacts have been found in contexts which are in any way associated with traces of domestic settlement; nevertheless, the distribution of such objects ought to reflect in general terms the areas of contemporary settlement. From about 1400 B.C., the main areas of settlement were southern Scotland and north-east Scotland as far north as the Moray Firth, broadly the same areas as indicated by Cinerary Urn burials. Beginning around the mid-eighth century B.C., the Scottish bronze industry underwent a considerable expansion, with large numbers of objects being produced and local specialisation of types. This need not imply a numerical growth of population, rather a technological development of the metal industry. The fact that many objects are found as hoards deliberately buried does, however, suggest a state of some unrest, and it is therefore significant that defensive forts and protective fenced settlements appear in the seventh century B.C.

These hill-forts, the defences of which are known to have incorporated a form of timber-lacing, were normally built of stone in Scotland; most have been identified by the visible masses of fused or vitrified stone which resulted from the firing of the timbers within them (either accidentally or as the result of enemy action). There may well be unburnt examples either in stone or earth which have yet to be discovered by excavation. The purpose of timber-lacing was to stabilise the loose rubble core and to prevent excessive pressure on the wall-face. The areas enclosed by these forts vary considerably, and so must the size of the communities that inhabited them. The range of artefacts found in the early examples of forts is limited to coarse pottery, jet rings, and stone tools, none of which are helpful in determining the cultural affinities of their inhabitants.

A continental origin for the timber-lacing technique has been an accepted assumption in archaeological thought for some years. Based on examples of timber-laced forts in northern Germany and Switzerland, which may be dated from the ninth century B.C. onwards, the idea that this technique was brought to Scotland from northern Europe found support in the contacts with that area which are evident in bronze artefacts dating from the seventh to the fifth century B.C. in Scotland. There are some 40 of these imported bronzes, but their distribution does not coincide significantly with that of timber-laced forts, thereby casting doubt on any primary connection between the two. The imported artefacts have been found predominantly along the north-east coast, a distribution which might be expected of trade with northern Europe. Most of the objects are swords and personal ornaments such as armlets, a fact which lends itself to two interpretations: it might suggest that the objects were brought to Scotland by their owners as personal luggage, or alternatively that a relatively wealthy society existed in Scotland at this time which had created a demand for luxury goods. Support for the latter interpretation is provided by examples of Irish gold imported in the seventh century, and by the fact that local industry had been stimulated to produce bronze swords and spearheads in the seventh and sixth centuries, the distribution of which coincides with that of timber-laced forts.

The most significant type of artefact in considering timber-laced forts ought to be the axe, for this tool must have been vitally necessary in order to cut the very large quantities of timber required. It has been estimated that about 640 young trees must have been felled in order to construct the fort at Abernethy in Perthshire, involving about 60 acres of natural forest – and this is only a small fort, enclosing an area about 135 by 45 ft. Radio-carbon dates indicate that some timber-laced forts were being constructed in the seventh century B.C., and it is therefore significant that the distribution of socketed bronze axes of that period correlates well with that of the forts. Some of these axes were imported from Ireland and England, but the majority represent local Scottish industry, copying imported objects.

These axes have also been found around the Tweed valley, where there is little evidence as yet of timber-lacing. The earliest enclosed settlements here are palisaded sites, which are apparently contemporary with timber-laced forts elsewhere, and which consist of one or more concentric lines of timber palisade enclosing a number of circular wooden houses. The axe would again be vitally important to their construction. In some cases, an outer line of fencing at some distance from the inner testifies to the importance of stock-rearing in the economy of the occupants, for a space was thus provided for penning animals. Few artefacts have been found on these sites, mainly coarse pottery and rough stone tools, and they cannot, on present evidence, be connected with influences from outside Scotland. As the earliest enclosed settlements in south-east Scotland, palisades are more likely to reflect the needs of a developing native society and economy rather than an alien tradition brought by invaders.

The introduction of iron-working in the mid-first millennium B.C. certainly suggests that at least one or two smiths emigrated to Scotland, and fortifications are certainly part of the 'Common Celtic' tradition. The crucial point is the introduction of the P-Celtic Gallo-Brittonic language, certainly established before the arrival of the Romans; a new language ought to involve immigration of people, but the precise date and context of the arrival in Scotland of P-Celtic speakers, the fourth strand in the make-up of the prehistoric population, cannot yet be determined – but arrive they did. There are, however, one or two major points of divergence between British and continental Celtic tradition, including the retention of the circular house-plan and the scarcity of formal burials and cemeteries in Britain, in contrast to the normal rectangular buildings and the abundant cemeteries on the continent.

Apart from timber-laced forts, there are numerous fortifications, particularly in south-east Scotland, dating from the middle and later first millennium B.C. These include stone-walled forts and forts with earthen ramparts; frequently a combination of the two on one site demonstrates the considerable length of time during which the forts were occupied. Excavation at Hownam Rings in Roxburghshire has indicated an apparently typical sequence of fortifications; a primary timber palisade was replaced by a single stone wall, itself replaced subsequently by a series of concentric earthen ramparts.

Most of these forts, apart from the late tribal centres, enclose only an acre or less of land, and it is often argued that they represent a fragmented society involving only very localised organisation. It is surely equally possible that overall tribal authority did exist but that, for some reason probably connected with economy, it was not embodied in any material way that would survive in the archaeological record.

Outlying barriers were sometimes employed to provide additional protection to forts. These take the form either of detached lengths of earthwork spanning the ridges along which access to the forts was obtained, or, occasionally, of *chevaux de frise,* large numbers of jagged stones set upright and close together immediately outside forts to impede attack. Both types of barrier are particularly suitable for defence against horse-borne warriors.

The fact that a number of forts remained unfinished has been attributed to Roman intervention, but there is as yet insufficient dating evidence for these structures to allow this idea to be more than an assumption. Unfinished forts can provide invaluable information about the way in which construction was undertaken, apparently by separate gangs of workmen set along a line marked out on the ground by means of a shallow trench.

In the late first millennium B.C. and the early first millennium A.D. the settlement pattern in the west and north of Scotland was quite distinct from that of the south and east; smaller units based on the fortified homestead, in various specialised forms, take the place of the hill-forts of the east. The simplest form is the 'dun', which is widespread in Argyll and Skye; these are round or D-shaped stone-walled structures, with an internal diameter of about 40 ft., the walls of which were strengthened in a few cases by timber-lacing. Some sites are situated in strong positions on rocky outcrops and on hill-tops, but their size is often equivalent only to that of one or two hut-platforms in the Lowlands. 'Brochs' represent sophisticated architectural concepts, involving a hollow-wall construction in order to achieve greater height; the well-known example of Mousa (Shetland) still stands to a height of over 40 ft. The broch is a peculiarly Scottish phenomenon which appears to have evolved from an earlier type of stone fort found on Skye, (although it has also been suggested that they originate in Orkney). The classic 'cooling-tower' profile and the two thicknesses of walling with narrow galleries between can be seen at two brochs in Glen Elg (Inverness-shire), and the simpler form of structure from which they may have evolved is visible further up the valley at Dun Grugaig. The flowering of broch architecture appears to date to about the last century B.C. and the first century A.D. In several cases, the broch formed the nucleus of a settlement which continued after the broch itself had gone out of use; the broch frequently became a quarry for stone, and later huts and cells were built within and around it, as at Gurness and Midhowe in Orkney. Some of these settlements continued into the Pictish period, for symbol stones have been found associated with several such post-broch occupations.

Apart from fortifications represented by hill-forts, duns and brochs, there are also non-defensive types of settlement belonging to the later first millennium B.C. These consist of circular stone-or timber-built houses, sometimes enclosed within low stone walls or earthen banks and sometimes standing free of any form of overall enclosure. The choice of stone or timber as building material was normally governed by available sources, but, in south-east Scotland at least, the use of timber for building houses predominated over stone until the first century A.D. Most stone-built houses in that area appear to belong to the Roman period.

Many of the most elaborate pieces of metalwork in the distinctive Celtic art-style were made for the warrior chieftain and his lady. The Celtic delight in ostentation which is illustrated in the later Irish tales finds its only archaeological expression in the flamboyant weapons, armlets, mirrors and torcs of the first few centuries A.D. Early Celtic art was European in origin with North Alpine, Classical and even Oriental elements in its make-up. The pieces found in Scotland are in some cases of English manufacture, like the torc terminal from Cairnmuir (Peeblesshire), the pony-cap and decorated horn-terminals from Torrs (Kirkcudbrightshire), and others of north British inspiration such as the sword scabbard from Mortonhall, Edinburgh. All, however, epitomise the colourful panoply of the Celtic warrior chief.

The warrior aristocracy in Scotland at the time of Mons Graupius used chariots, although they had already gone out of use in the rest of the Celtic world, except for Ireland. Two small horses, about the size of Exmoor ponies, pulled the chariot and they were guided by an able charioteer, who did not join in the battle. The chariot and the harness of the horses were probably elaborately ornamented and many examples of bridle-bits and harness-fittings have been found inlaid with enamel.

The principal weapons of the warriors were spears with iron tips, swords and shields; there is little evidence in Scotland of such defensive armour as helmets or mail (probably a Celtic invention), or of shields, because these were made of wood or leather and do not frequently survive. There are several elaborate scabbards or scabbard-terminals, like those from Glencotho and Mortonhall, decorated with tendril ornament and 'trumpet-coil' motifs. Perhaps the most exciting martial object in the Celtic art style is the mouth of a bronze trumpet in the shape of a boar from Deskford (Banffshire). Roman authors frequently mentioned the blowing of trumpets which preceded battle with the Celts, as well as their disconcerting battle cries.

Some of the most impressive pieces of Scottish Celtic art are neck ornaments and armlets decorated with bronze-beads and elaborate scroll and tendril motifs. Massive armlets and bracelets in the form of stylised snakes were manufactured in the north-east in the late first and early second centuries A.D. The cast armlets were ornamented with a series of ribs and tendrils, and, in some cases, the circular terminal was infilled with enamelled discs. The decoration on the collar from Stichill (Roxburghshire) is a more restrained example.

The Celts were accustomed to, and indeed enjoyed, inter-tribal warfare and raiding, but the fight for the survival of their way of life against organised Roman forces was something they were incapable of winning on the battlefield because of their lack of centralised political or military organisation.

One of the most tantalising aspects of Celtic archaeology is religion, for, although there is much to be learnt from contemporary

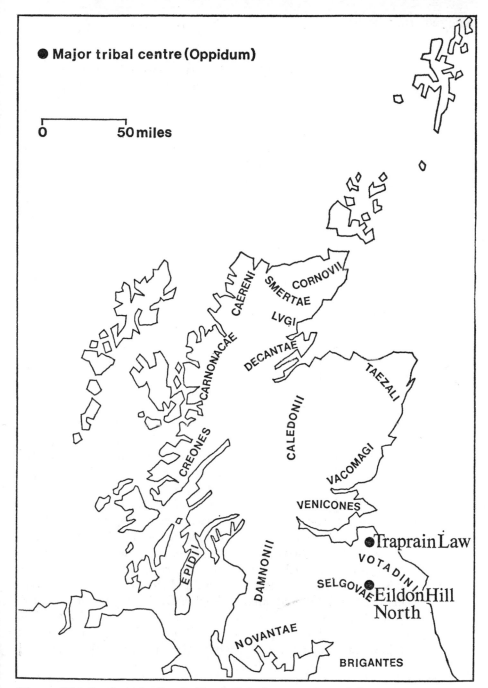

Major tribal centre (Oppidum)

0   50 miles

CORNOVII

SMERTAE

CAERENI

LVGI

DECANTAE

CARNONACAE

TAEZALI

CALEDONII

CREONES

VACOMAGI

VENICONES

●Traprain Law

EPIDII

VOTADINI

DAMNONII

SELGOVAE

●Eildon Hill
North

NOVANTAE

BRIGANTES

Fig 4   Distribution of tribes in North Britain around 100 A.D.

authors and by inference from later Irish epic tales, there are few material remains. Contemporary writers described the continental Celts as venerating pools and wells and worshipping their gods in groves of trees. Some temples are known on the Continent as in England but none has so far been firmly located in Scotland. The cult of the human head was one important facet of religion, however, and there are several stone heads including horned and possibly triple-headed examples from Scotland. Only in exceptional circumstances have wooden figures survived but there is one Scottish example from the peat-moss at North Ballachulish (Inverness-shire), where an austere oak idol was found in the remains of what may have been a small hut with wicker walls.

There is little direct evidence of the structure of Celtic society in Scotland but it is possible, from what is known of other areas, to infer a three-fold division within the tribe; the chieftain or 'king', a warrior aristocracy and with them a class of priests and poets, while below them was the main body of freemen. The existence of an unfree and virtually slave class is also thought to have existed in some areas. It is easy to imagine the smooth working of such a system in the east of Scotland where there are obvious tribal capitals such as the Votadinian *oppidum* of Traprain Law (East Lothian); in the west of Scotland, it is possible that, because of the difficulties of communication, the social structure was rather looser. It is likely, in any case, that the tribal units were smaller. The Greek geographer, Ptolemy, gives the names of some ten tribes in the Highland areas and seven, seemingly covering larger areas, in the Lowlands; the precise geographical positions of all the tribes are not, however, firmly established. The tribal pattern of the late first and second centuries A.D. is of interest as it mirrors to some extent the territorial divisions of the mid-first millennium A.D., with the Damnonii in the valley of the Clyde forming Strathclyde, the northern and eastern tribes becoming the main Pictish grouping, while the Votadini and the Selgovae were eventually overrun by the advancing Angles. Of the capitals and centres of the Celtic tribes, such as the Selgovae *oppidum* on Eildon Hill North, only Edinburgh, one of the centres of Votadinian power, retained any importance throughout the first millennium A.D.

CHAPTER III

The Roman Frontier

Anne S. Robertson

Attempts by the Romans to find a satisfactory frontier for the Roman province of Britannia spanned almost two centuries in time, and created a varying series of relationships between the Romans and the inhabitants of what is now called Scotland. Written records of these relationships all come from Roman sources, but even through 'the Roman version' there gleams part at least of 'the other side of the story'. Still more of that story can be pieced together from archaeological evidence, for example from Roman military structures, and contemporary native sites in North Britain, and from finds of Roman material on non-Roman sites.

The earliest Roman search for a frontier in North Britain was the work of Gnaeus Julius Agricola, governor of Britannia from A.D. 78–84, in the Flavian period (that period, A.D. 69–96, during the reign of the three emperors whose family name was Flavius). Agricola's search for a frontier influenced all subsequent Roman activity in North Britain, and his search is also the most fully documented. The biography of Agricola written by his son-in-law, the historian Tacitus, about A.D. 98, preserves a long account of Roman campaigns in North Britain between A.D. 80 and 84.

In A.D. 80 Agricola's army advanced from the Tyne-Solway isthmus through the territories of 'new tribes', until he reached the Taus estuary, which it is generally agreed must have been the Tay. The 'new tribes' were not named by Tacitus himself, but the lowland tribes at least can be identified from the early second century A.D. geographer Ptolemy (and his late first century sources), as the Votadini of Northumberland, Berwickshire and East Lothian, the Selgovae of the Central Lowlands and the Damnonii of Ayrshire, the Clyde Valley and part of Stirlingshire. To the territory of the Votadini Ptolemy assigned three place-names. One of them was Curia, a tribal hosting-place, which may have been the great oppidum of the Votadini on Traprain Law, East Lothian. To the Selgovae Ptolemy gave four place-names, three unlocated and the fourth Trimontium, the triple peak of the Eildon Hill, on the north side of which stood another great oppidum. The lands of the Damnonii included Vindogara on Irvine Bay.

Tribal oppida were gathering-places and market-towns to which came farmers, homesteaders, villagers and small townsfolk to exchange their produce for manufactured goods, and to hear the latest news. In and from the tribal oppida news of the Roman advance would spread like wildfire. In such tribal oppida if anywhere resistance to the Roman invader could have been organised and leaders have been found. Yet Tacitus states that 'the enemy', terror-stricken, did not dare to harry the Roman army as it swept northwards. There was even time for the building of forts, as distinct from the temporary camps constructed in the initial stages of the campaign. Such forts would lie along Agricola's main lines of advance so as to secure communications with the legionary fortresses at York and Chester, whence came the Ninth Legion and the Second Adiutrix and the Twentieth Legions, which, together with auxiliary, light-armed units, made up the invasion army. The distribution of such forts shows that Agricola used the two main natural routes from the south, the eastern route by way of the Tweed to the Forth, and the western route up Annandale to Upper Clydesdale, and thence north-eastwards to the Forth.

The most important Agricolan site in south Scotland was the great fort at Newstead on the Tweed, named Trimontium after triple-peaked Eildon Hill whose great oppidum it confronted. The tribal oppidum has not yet been excavated, but it has not so far yielded any chance Roman finds of the late first century A.D. It may either have been evacuated by the Romans, or have been abandoned by refugees fleeing before the Roman advance. A Roman signal tower placed at the west end of Eildon Hill may date to the Flavian period. In sharp contrast the Votadinian oppidum on Traprain Law continued in native occupation. Evidently its folk had succeeded in coming to some kind of terms with the Romans which enabled them to acquire late first century glass vessels and pottery.

From the Forth-Clyde isthmus to the Tay there was one single natural route, that imposed by the configuration of the country. Temporary camps lie along this route, on which in time there were also built permanent forts. The tribes through whose territory the Forth-Tay route must have passed were the Venicones and Vacomagi of Ptolemy. The territory of the Venicones included Fife. The Vacomagi lived further north in Strathmore and beyond.

In the next year Agricola's army made no further advance beyond the Tay, but took measures to secure the territories over-run, by road-building, fort-construction and the complete pacification of the lowlands. Those North Britons who came to terms with the Roman invader, like the folk of Traprain, could be left in peace, but irreconcilable elements would be exterminated or become homeless exiles. Where the intractable exiles fled to for refuge is indicated

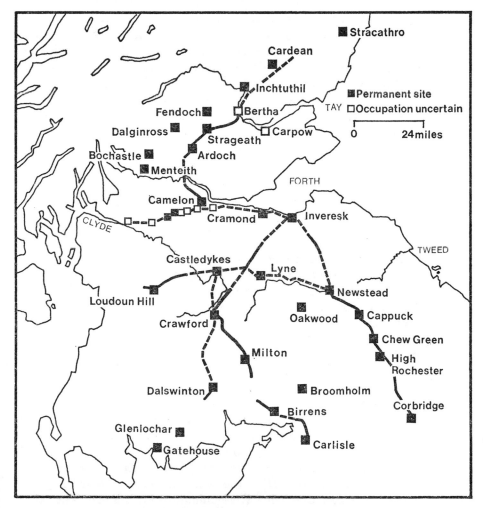

Fig 5   North Britain in the Flavian Period

both by Tacitus' narrative and by the location of Flavian forts on
and to the north of the Forth-Clyde isthmus. 'The estuaries of
Forth and Clyde,' said Tacitus, 'carried far inland by the tides
of opposite seas, are separated by but a narrow strip of land which
at this time was strengthened by garrisons (or small forts?), and
the whole tract of nearer country was held, the enemy being removed as it were into another island.' Several sites on the Forth-
Clyde isthmus, which were later occupied by forts on the Antonine
Wall, have revealed evidence for earlier occupation, probably of
the Flavian period. At Bar Hill and Croy Hill, two of the highest
sites on the isthmus, remains of small early forts, each with an
annexe, have been located. At four or five other isthmus sites
Flavian pottery and glassware have been found.

There was of course no Flavian frontier barrier on the Forth-
Clyde isthmus. Agricola, as Tacitus indicates, recognised the merit
of the isthmus as a frontier but disdained it so far as he was concerned. His frontier was to be the far northern sea, and his aim
was the complete conquest of Caledonia, a name used by Tacitus
to cover the whole highland region. Within it the tribe Caledonii
occupied territory extending from the Tay Valley to the Great
Glen.

North of the Forth-Clyde isthmus there was 'as it were another
island'. The pattern of Roman forts north of the isthmus demonstrates that hostile elements were to be forced back into their own
mountains west of the Roman route from Forth to Tay, and to be
kept there by forts blocking the exits to mountain passes, of which
four are now known – at Menteith, Bochastle near Callander,
Dalginross and Fendoch. Behind this cordon of Roman forts the
North Britons watched and waited and prepared their final resistance against the invader. The Romans too kept watch, from
their forts, and probably from a line of small wooden signal towers
on the Gask ridge between Strageath and Perth.

In the next year, A.D. 82, Agricola, according to Tacitus, 'subdued tribes hitherto unknown in several successful battles, having
crossed over (somewhere) in the leading ship, and having placed
troops in that part of Britain which looks towards Ireland'. Of
the tribes hitherto unknown one must have been the Novantae of
Galloway and lands west of the Nith, in whose territory Ptolemy
named two sites, one being Rerigonium on Loch Ryan. The other
new tribe may have been the Damnonii. It may have been in this

year rather than in A.D. 80 that Agricola's army laid out the western route from Carlisle to the Upper Clyde Valley and thence to the Forth, and the cross-road from Newstead on the Tweed via Castledykes on the Clyde towards Loudoun Hill in Ayrshire. Evidently the west end of the cross-road was making for a port on the Ayrshire coast, possibly near Ardrossan. No remains of a Flavian port or fort on the Ayrshire coast have yet been found, but Flavian pottery from a native dwelling-site at Glenhead, near Ardrossan, was probably acquired from a nearby Roman site, possibly on the north side of Irvine Bay (the Vindogara of Ptolemy).

Some of the Damnonii lived in crannogs or lake-dwellings. One of these at least, at Hyndford, near Lanark, has its occupation dated to this period by the presence of Roman glassware, and pottery, all of Flavian types. If this was acquired peacefully through trade with the nearby Roman fort at Castledykes it may suggest that some of the Clyde Valley folk at least went over to the Roman side without a struggle. The Novantae on the other hand probably gave more trouble. In their territory Flavian forts cluster close.

The scene of Agricola's crossing may have been the Solway, and the part of Britain looking towards Ireland would include south-west Scotland and the Cumberland coast. The 'crossing' was not a crossing to Ireland. The only Roman discoveries in Ireland are of moveable finds, usually coins and a little pottery, which had been taken over the Irish Sea by way of trade.

It may be that in A.D. 82 Agricola's fleet sailed among the Western Isles, for the second century geographer Ptolemy knew the names of several west-coast tribes: the Epidii ('horse-folk') of Kintyre, the Cerones ('folk of the rough lands') further north, the Carnonacae ('folk of the cairns or rocky hills') of Wester Ross, the Caereni of north-west Sutherland, and the Cornavii ('folk of the promontory') of Caithness. The initial campaigns of Agricola had aroused the 'Caledonian confederacy' which included also the Taezali of the extreme north-east, the Decantae ('noble-folk') of Easter Ross, the Lugi ('raven-folk') of Sutherland, and the Smertae, between the Lugi and Caereni. Some of these folk at least had been threatening the Roman line from the Forth to the Tay.

In A.D. 83 therefore Agricola enveloped the area north of the Forth, and made considerable use of his fleet. His land army advanced in three columns, according to Tacitus, and the enemy struck by concentrating a night attack on the Ninth Legion as being the weakest. An inscription proves that in this year a detachment from this legion was taking part in the operations of the emperor Domitian against the Chatti across the Upper Rhine. Evidently the fact that the Ninth Legion was not at full strength was no secret to the North Britons! Agricola's advanced campaigning base would by now have been at Inchtuthil, where a great legionary fortress may already have been a-building. An advance in three columns on a broad front would suit Strathmore, five miles wide, with the flanks of the advancing force along the foothills of the Perthshire Grampians and the Sidlaws.

In his final campaign, in A.D. 84, Agricola sent his fleet ahead on a series of harassing forays, with the aim of forcing the enemy to make a stand in a pitched battle. His army, which now included some Britons (from the south) used the same line of advance as in A.D. 83, from Inchtuthil through Strathmore and Kincardine into Aberdeenshire, until his way was barred by a Caledonian army drawn up on the slopes of Mons Graupius. The battle was fought somewhere near an entrenched position, that is a Roman camp, and Tacitus seems to imply that it was the furthest north point reached by Agricola. The final Roman advance then may be supposed to have led from Aberdeenshire towards Inverness, by way of Keith commanding the Pass of Grange, between the Grampians and the Knock Hill group, which opens on the lower Spey and the lowlands about Elgin and Nairn. Near Keith it may be the 'Caledonians' were waiting with a line of retreat through Dufftown into the Highlands.

According to Tacitus 'the strength of all the tribes' amounting to 30,000 men had been summoned. Native structures north of the Forth proved by Roman material found in them to have been in use during the late first century A.D. include a homestead, a dun, a stack-fort and a broch. From dwellings such as these there flocked in a large army, among whose leaders the most outstanding was Calgacus ('the swordsman'). The speech which Tacitus puts into the mouth of Calgacus represents an intellectual Roman interpretation of the 'Caledonian' view of the Roman invasion. 'They make a desert place and call it peace' is only one of its memorable phrases. Tacitus also gave Agricola a speech justifying the Roman policy of conquest. Mons Graupius marked yet another Roman victory. The losses according to Tacitus were 10,000 of the 'enemy' and 360 Romans.

After the battle Agricola led his troops down into the territory of the Boresti, probably in the lowlands of the Moray Firth. He then ordered his fleet to sail round Britain, thus proving it to be an island. In the course of the voyage the fleet subdued the Orkney Islands and saw Thule (the Shetlands). His army made a land journey to quarters in the south. In A.D. 84–85 Agricola's governorship of Britain came to an end.

Meanwhile the native survivors of Mons Graupius had melted away again into the Highlands. Agricola's plan, however, for the consolidation of the conquest remained in operation. Its aim was to isolate the Highlands by blocking exits from the passes, and to establish a major striking force in a legionary fortress at Inchtuthil with a screen of auxiliary forts to the north of it, of which two are known, at Cardean and Stracathro. The road system and forts from Tay to Forth, and forts on the two main routes through south Scotland and on the cross-road continued in use, with other forts on spur-roads at Oakwood and Broomholm. The small posts on the Forth-Clyde isthmus may have had a shorter life.

The Agricolan plan for North Britain justifies the Tacitean phrase – Britannia perdomita ('Britain thoroughly conquered'). But 'et statim amissa' ('and immediately given up') followed. The plan had to be abandoned because shattering Roman defeats on the Danube required the withdrawal of one of the four legions stationed in Britain, perhaps as early as A.D. 86. As a result, the legionary fortress at Inchtuthil was given up, before building had been completed and soon after the date of its six latest coins, all newly minted bronze Asses of A.D. 86. This involved also the evacuation of auxiliary forts to the north, and possibly, of all the Flavian forts in North Britain except for the great fort at Newstead on the Tweed. This fort seems to have been held longer than the rest, perhaps until about A.D. 100.

For the decades following Agricola's governorship in North Britain there is an almost complete lack of literary evidence. Archaeological evidence from the native side suggests, however, that the withdrawal of Roman garrisons encouraged a freer movement of native peoples. This resulted, for example, in the building of brochs far from the broch province, for example at Hurly Hawkin, Angus, and at Torwoodlee, Selkirkshire. At both these sites, the broch had been built within or over an earlier native fort, and both sites yielded Flavian pottery.

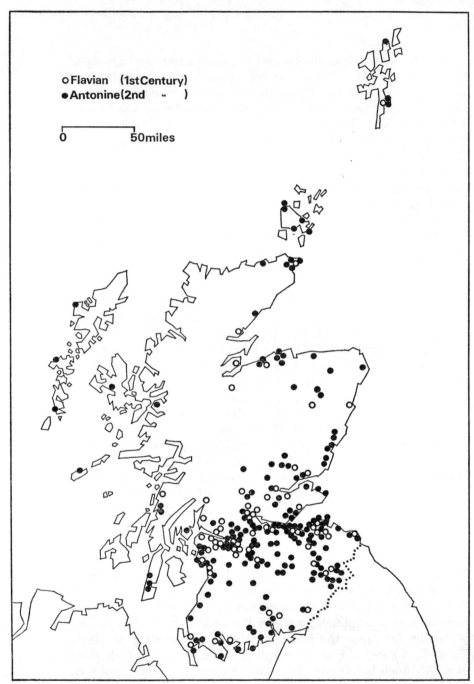

Fig 6   *Roman finds from non-Roman sites (1st & 2nd centuries A.D.)*

It is probable too that these decades marked an influx of new settlers into south-west Scotland. The hill-fort on Birrenswark Hill, Dumfriesshire, may have been constructed at this time. Some of the folk of south-west Scotland even threatened the peace of the Roman province of Britannia which now received its first continuous frontier barrier, Hadrian's Wall, running from the Tyne to the Solway, with outlying forts in the west at Birrens, Netherby and Bewcastle. So fierce and unrelenting was the pressure of the south-western folk on Hadrian's Wall that less than 20 years after it was built the emperor Antoninus Pius had to move the frontier northwards to the Forth-Clyde isthmus, the old east-west line which Agricola had strengthened with small forts 60 years earlier.

The land between the Tyne-Solway and the Forth-Clyde isthmus was contained and added to the Roman empire. The only literary evidence is one sentence by a late third century writer, Capitolinus, *Vita Antonini Pii*, 'For he (i.e. the emperor Antoninus Pius) conquered the Britons through Lollius Urbicus the governor (i.e. of Britain) and after driving back the barbarians, built another wall, this time of turf.' Bronze coins of Antoninus Pius commemorate the victory won in North Britain. They have on the reverse side the figure of Britannia subdued, in the guise of a female figure seated left, with her head leaning on her right hand in the conventional attitude of mourning or subjection, and her left arm resting on a great spiked shield. These coins, minted in late A.D. 142, or early A.D. 143, determine the date of Lollius Urbicus' campaigns in North Britain and also provide an approximate date for the building of the Antonine Wall which followed swiftly thereafter.

The army of Lollius Urbicus doubtless moved northwards along the same two main natural routes into Scotland which Agricola had laid out 60 years before – one route by way of the Tweed and Lauderdale to the Forth, and the other by Annandale and Upper Clydesdale. Lower Clydesdale, however, featured in the Antonine system, although not apparently in the Flavian road system. In the Antonine period, forts were in time built not only at Castledykes near Lanark, but also at Bothwellhaugh near Hamilton. A road linked these forts and must have continued north towards the west end of the Forth-Clyde isthmus.

The troublesome North Britons were once again pushed back into their own mountains, and a penetrative road, guarded by forts, was driven far into Perthshire. The irreconcilable elements

in south-west Scotland in particular were kept in check by a network of roads, forts and fortlets, probably linked with a harbour
on the Solway. The cross-road from Newstead via Lyne and Castledykes past Loudoun Hill indicates that there was once more a
Roman port on the Ayrshire coast, probably on Irvine Bay. The
breaking up of disaffected elements in south Scotland may have
led to the deportation of some irreconcilables to the Roman frontier
on the Rhine, where units of Britons have recorded their presence
on inscriptions of Antonine date. It may have been now that the
hill-fort on Birrenswark Hill was evacuated. It may even be that

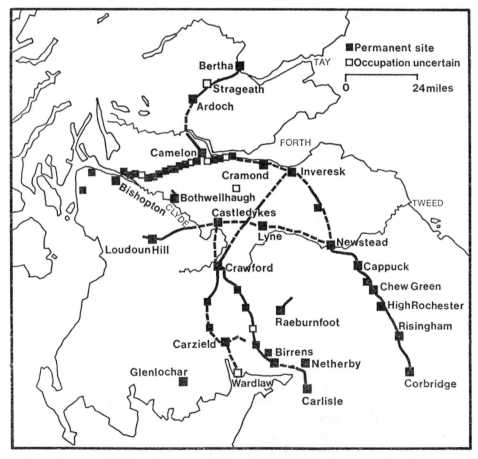

Fig 7   North Britain in the Antonine Period

the lonely little Roman fort of Raeburnfoot, Eskdalemuir, with its very large compound, and apparently short life, belonged to an early Antonine phase when prisoners were being rounded up and placed in 'concentration camps'.

The Antonine Wall itself was built from Bridgeness on the Forth to Old Kilpatrick on the Clyde, a distance of about 37 miles. For most of its length it clung to the southern slopes of the isthmus valley with a clear view across the valley to the threatening hills on the north. The Wall was constructed of turves, as the Roman writer said, underpinned by a stone base, not less than 14 ft. wide. To the north of the Wall there ran a Ditch, about 40 ft. wide and 12 ft. deep. To the south of the Wall at an average distance of 40–50 yards, there ran a cambered road, the Military Way, 16–18 ft. wide. The construction of the Antonine frontier was carried out by working squads from the Second, Sixth and Twentieth Legions. They were doubtless protected while at work by units of light-armed auxiliary troops and they may have had enforced assistance in the unskilled tasks of fetching and carrying by native North Britons.

There have been recovered from the line of the Antonine Wall eighteen 'distance slabs' set up by legionary working squads to commemorate the distance or length of the Wall which they had completed. Several of them represent conquered North Britons, kneeling with their hands tied behind them. The most remarkable of the known distance slabs was found as recently as 1969, on Hutcheson Hill, west of Castlehill, Bearsden. It records the completion of 3,000 ft. of the Wall by a detachment of the Twentieth Legion. The inscription has been arranged within an architectural framework representing either a triumphal arch or the shrine of the standards. The central niche or panel encloses a female figure holding out a little wreath to a legionary eagle held by an aquilifer. The panels on either side contain kneeling captives.

On the line of the Antonine Wall forts were built very close together, at 2-mile intervals. They were situated on ground which in Roman times afforded a very wide outlook to north and usually in all directions. It seems virtually certain that the building of the Wall itself was begun from the east, and that some sites at least in the western sector had forts built on them before the Wall arrived. Evidently a watchful control had to be maintained over the restless resentful North Britons to the north of the west end of the Wall while its building was in progress.

Between at least three pairs of Antonine Wall forts there were built small interval-fortlets. One of these, between Falkirk and Rough Castle, stood at a check-point where a major Roman road passed through the frontier northwards in the direction of the forts at Camelon and Ardoch. At certain places on the line small turf signalling-platforms were attached to the rear of the Wall. Three pairs of such platforms are known, one pair to east and one pair to west of the fort at Rough Castle, and another pair on the western slope of Croy Hill. At only two points had the Antonine Wall to be carried across rivers of any size – the Avon near its east end and the Kelvin near its west end. The Kelvin crossing was guarded by the great stone-walled fort of Balmuildy which over-looked a wooden bridge on stone piers. The Avon crossing was watched by a small fort at Inveravon, on the east bank.

The Romans had also to guard against enemy landings on the south banks of the Forth and Clyde. The danger was lessened on

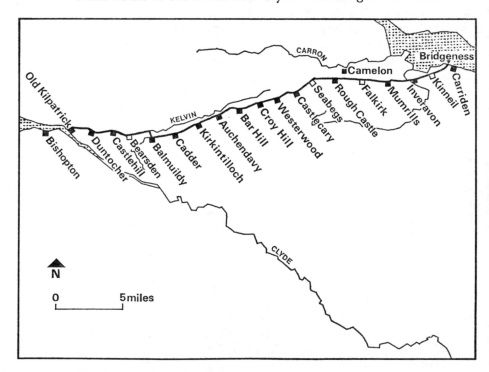

Fig 8   The Antonine Wall

the Forth by the existence of a Roman road running along its south bank from Inveresk through Cramond, where there was a harbour, to the east end of the Wall. Attempts by North Britons to land on the south bank of the Clyde were anticipated and provided against by a fort at Whitemoss, Bishopton, just over 2 miles as the crow flies from the west end of the Antonine Wall, and by at least two fortlets, on Lurg Moor, above Greenock, and at Outerwards, above Largs. These kept watch on the coasts of the Firth of Clyde.

A North Briton who made his way south through a gap in the hills on the north side of the isthmus, like the Blane Valley, and looked towards the southern scarp, would see, running east and west for mile after mile, the great barrier of the Wall itself, towering up with its wooden breastwork, to a height not far short of 20 ft., and the deep ravine of the Ditch in front. His eye would pick out the forts, close-set at intervals of about every 2 miles, between which patrols carried out their ceaseless vigil along the rampart-walk on top of the Wall. As his gaze strained hopefully, or despairingly, westwards beyond the west end of the Wall itself, there would come into view the Roman harbour below Old Kilpatrick, busy with Roman shipping, and the Roman stations along the south bank of the Clyde. Even a distant view of the great frontier would impress the native beholder with a sense of his own helplessness against the power and majesty of Rome.

Britons who lived in occupied territory seem to have accepted the situation, and even to have turned it to their material advantage. As long as the Romans held the Antonine Wall, there was a steady 'drift' of Roman coins and other objects to native sites – crannogs, caves, huts, souterrains, enclosed settlements and the great oppidum of Traprain Law, still preserving its modus vivendi with the Romans. The most valuable Roman goods (like gold and silver coins, bronze vessels and brooches) evidently remained in Roman occupied territory in south Scotland, while a little of the more everyday material – glass bottles, beads, pottery – penetrated either by land or sea to the duns and brochs of the north and west. The latter may perhaps represent interchange between tribal peoples rather than direct contact between Roman and native. Contact between Roman and native took its most friendly form in the annexes attached to Roman forts on the Antonine Wall and in south Scotland. In time there grew up alongside these Antonine forts settlements of traders and civilians, some of them women and children. One settlement at least at Carriden at the east end of the Wall attained the status of a vicus, i.e. a recognised village community.

The Antonine system in North Britain lasted for 40–50 years. During that period, the Wall served as a base for military operations, with a line of outpost forts running to the gate of the Scottish Highlands. It also formed a physical and psychological barrier separating the tribes north of the Forth-Clyde line from Roman-protected territory to the south.

At the beginning of the third century A.D. Hadrian's Wall was restored as the frontier of Britannia, and the emperor Severus crossed to Britain to prepare for campaigns against the Caledonians, one of the two strongest tribes in North Britain, the other being the Maeatae, according to the third century writer Dio Cassius. Before the Caledonian campaigns, Severus 'bought peace from the Maeatae'. Early Severan coin hoards found in the eastern counties of Scotland north of the Forth may represent part of the purchase price.

Severus' campaigns against the Caledonians took place in A.D. 209–211. His army may have been transported by sea from South Shields at the mouth of the Tyne to the fort and harbour of Cramond on the Forth, and to Carpow on the Tay, where a legionary base was constructed. According to Dio Cassius, Severus reached the extremity of the island (probably the Moray Firth). That he followed the same route as Agricola is suggested by the series of large temporary camps in the north-east. He forced the Caledonians to come to terms, but trouble broke out again with both Caledonians and Maeatae. In A.D. 211, Severus died at York, and his son Caracalla quickly concluded the Caledonian campaigns, and returned to Rome. Hadrian's Wall remained the frontier of the Roman province for the next two centuries, with outpost forts at Netherby, Bewcastle, High Rochester and Risingham.

In the third century these forts accommodated not only infantry cohorts with cavalry contingents, but also units of irregulars who operated as long-range scouts, or *exploratores,* far to the north of Hadrian's Wall. In this century some of the souterrain folk of Angus, who may have been included among the Maeatae, moved into south Scotland. Some of them used Roman carved stones in the construction of souterrains at Crichton (Midlothian), and near

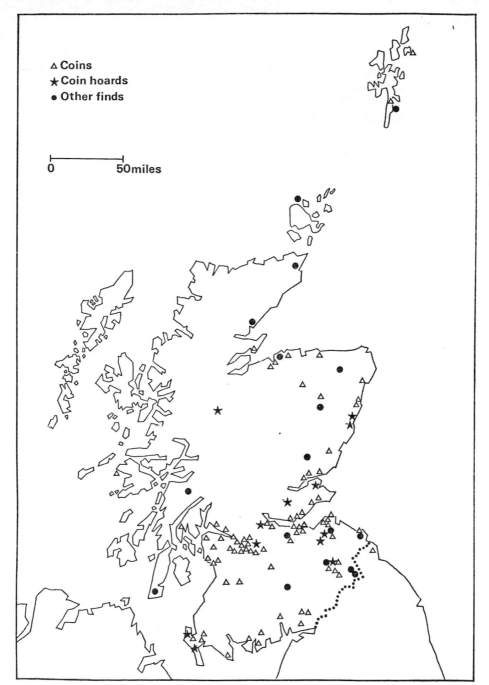

Fig 9   Roman finds from non-Roman sites (3rd and 4th centuries A.D.)

Newstead (Roxburghshire), and apparently even incorporated Roman tombstones into a souterrain at Shirva near the Antonine Wall. In this century too, several of the great hill-forts of south Scotland, formerly evacuated as a result of Roman invasions, had native villages built over their defences. Some of these villagers may have been among the *areani* (mentioned by Ammianus Marcellinus) or 'homesteaders' who seem to have replaced the exploratores as scouts in the fourth century A.D., until there came the 'barbarica conspiratio' of A.D. 367, a barbarian plan for a concerted attack on Britain. The subsequent 'restoration' of Count Theodosius transformed the tribes of the forward areas north of Hadrian's Wall into foederati ('treaty states').

In the third and fourth centuries A.D. Roman coins and other objects continued to reach Traprain Law in a steady flow. To other North British sites they came intermittently, some of them at least as the result of forays into the Roman province of Britannia.

On this, the most north-westerly frontier of the Roman Empire, the Roman army left to later centuries a permanent legacy, both through its relationships with the native peoples – which ranged from conquest and deportation, to re-settlement, trade and even intermarriage – and through its system of roads and forts. The road system offered convenient routes to contemporary and to post-Roman travellers, and accelerated the movement and intermingling of peoples in the early centuries of the Christian era. The massive Roman forts remained a familiar feature of the post-Roman landscape, and provided shelter for folk otherwise homeless. Almost every Roman fort-site in North Britain has produced medieval pottery left behind by such visitors. The Antonine Wall, in particular, stood century after century, serving as a boundary, a march or a trysting-place.

CHAPTER IV

The Problem of the Picts

Isabel Henderson

The one thing that most people know about the Picts is that together with the Scots they resisted the Romans so successfully that the Romans had to build Hadrian's Wall to keep them out of the province of Britain. Fortunately, this is probably the best starting point for an account of the Picts. The first reference to a people of this name living in North Britain is found in a panegyric poem written by an anonymous Roman towards the end of the third century A.D., at the time when Constantius Chlorus had succeeded in repairing the Wall after it had been overrun and destroyed by the northern tribes. The name is found regularly thereafter in classical and medieval writers.

Only a few years after this first reference another Roman writes of 'the woods and marshes of the *Caledones* and other Picts' and this suggests that the single tribe, the *Caledones*, was part of a larger whole called 'Picts'. In the fourth century the Picts are said to have been divided into two peoples. This may be an over-simplification, but again it is clear that 'Picts' is being used as a collective name for the inhabitants of North Britain. Roman writers also used 'Caledonians' as a collective name for these tribes, by extension from the single tribe of that name. The *Caledonii* appear on Ptolemy's map, occupying a large territory stretching from the Beauly Firth to southern Perthshire. Ptolemy's information for North Britain came from sources that belong to the first century A.D., and it includes the names of a dozen or so tribes who lived north of the Forth-Clyde line – the southern boundary of the historical kingdom of the Picts. None of these tribes is called *Picti* and this suggests that the name only existed as a collective name. It may, in fact, simply have been a Roman nickname, 'the painted people', – a comment on their habit of painting and tattooing themselves. It could also be a translation of a very early British collective name, *Pritani*, which may mean 'the people of the designs', and which came to be used in the form *Priteni* to refer exclusively to the peoples north of the Forth. *Priteni* is a P-Celtic name, that is to say it belongs to the British dialect of Celtic. When this word was used by Q-Celtic speakers, those who spoke the Irish dialect of Celtic, it had to become *Cruithni* because Irish Celtic has no *p*. It is worth mentioning this because when reading about the Picts one may sometimes find them referred to as the *Cruithni*.

Who were these tribes whose names have been recorded by Ptolemy? What sort of lives did they live, what sort of houses and fortifications did they build? Previous chapters in this book will have explained how difficult it is to answer these questions. Archaeological studies in Scotland are at present engaged in coming to terms with the recent discovery, due to radio-carbon dating techniques, that the timber-framed forts (often called 'vitrified forts' because of the fusion of the stonework that occurred when the walls were burned) found in eastern Scotland, belong, not as had been thought to around 100 B.C., but to as early as the seventh century B.C. This discovery has naturally seriously disturbed interpretations of what was happening in North Britain at the time of Ptolemy's tribes. The significance attached to the evolution and adoption of the broch-tower has also been affected, for being roughly contemporary with the vitrified forts as originally dated the builders of the two types of structure were inevitably thought to stand in some relation to each other. These matters concern deeply the probable make-up of what can be called the proto-Pictish culture.

Writers on the Picts have been at pains to emphasise the probability that the peoples lumped together by the Romans under the name 'Picts' had a mixed racial and cultural background, in order to stress, correctly, that there is no trace of the *Picti* having arrived at some point in time to settle in North Britain in the way that the Scots arrived in Argyll and the Anglo-Saxon peoples arrived in the south. For reasons that will be given later the concept of a mixed cultural background for the Picts must be sustained but it should be noted that archaeologists are at present feeling their way towards the definition of what may be a single proto-Pictish culture for at least a large part of the Pictish area, whatever its later superficial tribal and political fragmentation.

Even if, however, we confine ourselves to the period after the appearance of the collective name 'Picts' there is not, as yet, a great deal of help to be had from archaeology in defining the nature of the culture of the people who lived in the north from the fourth century. Only a few instances of surface dwellings beside the underground structures known as souterrains bring us within sight of the historical period. The material culture of the souterrain builders, who were flourishing in the second and third centuries, is disappointingly meagre, and it has not been possible to estimate their role in proto-Pictish affairs. There is in general a great dearth of settlement sites from the fourth century onwards so that the opportunity of moving from the series of sites known to belong to the historical period back into prehistory is not available. It is true that one type of fort that belongs to the Dark Age period has been identified, and some examples, as at Moncrieffe Hill (Perthshire), are found in the Pictish area, but finds from these sites too have so far been small and unilluminating.

It has been necessary to touch on these matters to explain why the nature of the often-asked question 'Who were the Picts?' is unsatisfactory. It should be re-phrased as 'Who made up the Picts?', a form of question that underlines the fact that the Picts are composite and that a number of different answers is anticipated. At present we can point to the builders of the vitrified forts, whose ancient culture may have persisted right down to the historical period, the builders of the brochs and wheelhouses, themselves originally a mixed culture of incoming Celts and indigenous natives, and the souterrain builders, who may simply represent a development of the old vitrified fort culture. There are also other strands of archaeological evidence for the arrival of small groups of settlers but they need not concern us here.

Finding links between the prehistoric and the historical period is a major problem in Pictish studies. One satisfactorily strong link is found in the language spoken by the inhabitants of the north. In his classic review of the evidence for Pictish language Professor Kenneth Jackson was able to analyse names from classical writers and from early medieval sources contemporary with the historical Picts. The evidence from both periods was found to be consistent, and it is further confirmed by the modern place-names found in the Pictish area.

Professor Jackson shows that there were Celtic speakers in the Orkneys in the first century B.C. and possibly from as early as the fourth. There are many Celtic names in Ptolemy's map, which as we have seen, is relevant for the end of the first century A.D. A significant number of these names are P-Celtic, while none of them can be positively said to be Q-Celtic. The P-Celtic, however, is not absolutely identical with the Celtic spoken by the Britons but may perhaps have affinities with Gaulish. Celtic speakers therefore may have arrived in the north either directly from Gaul or from southern England during the last few centuries B.C. when the Celts there would have spoken a language akin to that of Gaul. By the turn of the Christian era this early Celtic in southern England was overlaid by the Brittonic speech of the later phase of Celtic arrivals. The archaeological background of the broch builders suggests that they would have spoken Brittonic but the later evidence and the place-names show that this Gallo-Brittonic Celtic prevailed in the historical period. It used to be speculated, for a number of good reasons, that the vitrified fort builders provided a suitable archaeological context for the Gallo-Brittonic speakers but the back-dating of the forts rules this out and an archaeological setting has yet to be found for them.

Professor Jackson not only found evidence for Gallo-Brittonic speakers but also for a population that spoke a non-Celtic, indeed non-Indo-European language. This he concludes must have been the language spoken by the indigenous tribes. The indications of this are clearly seen in Ptolemy's map where the names of the four chief tribes who occupy the main Pictish area, the *Caledonii, Vacomagi, Taezali* and *Venicones* are by no means clearly Celtic. Traces of this non-Celtic language are found in the historical part of the list of the kings of the Picts, and the Pictish Ogam inscriptions are written in it entirely.

The linguistic make-up of Britain north of the Forth-Clyde line seems, therefore, on the basis of the available evidence, to have been the same from at least the beginning of the Christian era, and the fact that two languages were apparently spoken in Pictland has to be taken into account at all periods. The answer then to another frequent question, 'Were the Picts Celtic?' is 'Partially so'. And to the further question, 'What sort of Celtic did they speak?' the answer is that it was akin to British Celtic but not exactly like it, having sufficient associations with Gaulish to justify its being given the name *Gallo-Brittonic*. When these facts are appreciated it is not difficult to see why we should expect to find Pictish culture and society significantly different from that of their Celtic-speaking neighbours, the Scots of Dalriada and the Britons of Strathclyde.

The differences indeed must have been very considerable for the evidence does not suggest that the non-Indo-European speakers became a subject population living under the rule of the Celts. The fact that this aboriginal language survived at all implies that the pre-Celtic element was strong. The most striking confirmation of this is the fact that the incoming Celts adopted the indigenous custom of matrilinear succession. Matrilinearism is not found in other Celtic societies and it would seem that the newcomers failed to impose their own law of succession on a population that outnumbered them. Bede, writing in the first half of the eighth century, says that the Pictish custom of choosing their kings from the female royal lineage was well known in his day, and the evidence of the list of the Pictish kings taken in conjunction with the kings' obits in the Irish Annals shows that the rule that a son should not succeed his father was strictly maintained.

The evidence for the Pictish law of inheritance through the female comes from historical sources but there is also perhaps some indirect evidence for it from an earlier period in the somewhat sensational accounts of Caledonian sexual practices found in classical writers. Dio Cassius, who wrote in the third century A.D., records an interesting conversation on this matter between a Roman matron and the wife of a Caledonian chief. When the Roman lady expresses her surprise at the flagrant promiscuity of Caledonian women, the chief's wife replies with dignity that theirs is the better way, to give themselves openly to the best men, rather than as Roman women do, to let themselves be debauched in secret by the vilest. 'Such', writes Dio, 'was the retort of the Caledonian woman.' It is clear that the Caledonians had some kind of polyandrous society perhaps of the type where a woman has a legal husband but where her other sexual partners have a recognised and respectable status. Matrilinearism is frequently found with polyandry as an obvious solution to the difficulty of proving paternity. To the observers on the other side of the Wall these subtleties would have been lost and an impression given of untrammelled licence.

These same classical writers were also greatly fascinated by the way in which the northern tribes painted and tattooed themselves. The word 'Picti' itself may, as we have seen, be a reference to this habit. Many writers refer specifically to this custom, often in terms of tattooing rather than mere daubing with colour in the manner of Caesar's Britons. It is true that much of this evidence is second hand but there seems no reason to doubt that the Picts, quite far on into the Roman period, liked to decorate themselves in this way. It is impossible to tell when or where the habit originated. The *Pritani* of South Britain may themselves have got their 'designs' from an older population and the habit moved north with the Celts and hung on there. Alternatively the older population in the north may have had its own tattooing traditions. Why they did it is not clear either. The motives for tattooing are broadly, magical, to keep off sickness and wounds, to indicate caste or rank, or most common of all, simply to decorate. Isidore of Seville, writing soon after A.D. 600, writes that the Pictish aristocracy tattooed itself 'ad sui specimen', but whether this should be translated simply as 'in a manner appropriate to itself' or more particularly as 'according to the personal rank of the individual', as some scholars have thought, is a matter of opinion. Professor Charles Thomas has suggested that the tattoo designs referred to by classical writers are the same as the symbolic designs used by the Picts, mainly on stone monuments, throughout the historical period. If this were so then we should have another very impressive link between the proto-Pictish and Pictish period proper.

The Pictish historical period really begins with the coming of Christianity around 565. By this time the situation in the north was such as to allow the king whom Columba visited, Bridei, son of Maelcon, to control the Orkneys from his royal residence near Loch Ness. Roman pressure, and later, the failure to dislodge the Scottish settlement of Argyll in the fifth century, must have stimulated a will to unite for the common good. According to Adomnan in his *Life of Columba*, written towards the end of the seventh century, Bridei controlled the Orkneys by holding hostages, and presumably this would be how he kept control over other districts as well. Bede called him a 'most powerful king' but it is not known how far south his kingdom extended. There is no evidence for any other Pictish king having been influential during his long reign, but in 584 he died fighting in a civil war in a district of southern Pictland and this may mean that the south wished to maintain a measure of independence.

Adomnan gives us a glimpse into Bridei's court, or at least a picture of what he thought was an appropriate setting for him. He gives Bridei a council, a priesthood, slaves (one of whom at least is Irish), messengers on horseback and a royal treasury. The chief priest is said to have been the *nutricius* of the king. This means 'foster-father' and it would seem, therefore, that the Picts practised the Celtic custom of 'fosterage', a system whereby the children of noble families were sent away from home to be brought up. In his journeying among the Picts Columba is said twice to have witnessed Picts being buried. This is interesting because so little is known about Pictish burial customs of any period. A Pictish household is described as comprising husband and wife, children and servants – an orderly and devoted group that comes as a surprise after the lurid reports in classical writers. One Pict is described as a 'captain of a cohort', a title that has yet to be satisfactorily explained. Certainly Bridei must have had an efficient army and fleet.

Even allowing for an element of anachronism, Adomnan's picture of Pictish society shows that by the sixth century the Picts had developed into a coherent people led by a typical Dark Age monarch who had all the resources of his foreign contemporaries. The Picts are referred to regularly in the written sources of these contemporaries and it should be stressed that there is never any suggestion in these sources that the Picts were regarded as a backward or in any way peculiar people. This contrasts strongly with the accounts given of them by classical writers who clearly, perhaps largely through ignorance and lack of sympathy, found them very alien.

In the years that followed the introduction of Christianity the Pictish kingdom undoubtedly comprised all the districts north of the Forth-Clyde line and was ruled by one king based in southern Pictland. Like their neighbours the Scots and the Britons, the Picts suffered from Northumbrian aggression from the middle of the seventh century. Eventually the Scots and Britons had to acknowledge the English as their overlords and pay them some kind of tribute. The Picts fared worse, actually losing some of their territory in the south. This period of the occupation by the English cannot have been all loss for it brought the Picts into close contact with the Northumbrians politically and ecclesiastically at a period when they were in the midst of an intellectual and artistic flowering of a remarkable kind. In the end the Picts from the north won a great victory over the Northumbrians in 685 at Dunnichen (Nechtansmere) in Angus. By this victory the Picts regained the southern part of their kingdom and released the Scots and the Britons from their obligations to the English. In 685 there is no doubt that the Picts were politically the most important people in North Britain. At this time it has been suggested, with some probability, that the Picts re-defined their frontier with the Scots, giving to the Scots, in exchange perhaps for Scottish settlements in Perthshire, all the land to the west of Druimalban. This was the boundary between the two peoples at the time when Adomnan was writing his *Life of Columba* very shortly after the victory of 685.

The political confidence gained at the end of the seventh century together with the prolonged contact with the Northumbrians may account for a major change in Pictish affairs taking place at the beginning of the following century on the initiative of the reigning king. Bede records that about 710 King Nechton sent messengers to Abbot Ceolfrith of Jarrow, in Northumbria, asking him to send convincing arguments for the adoption of Roman methods of calculating the date of Easter and other Roman customs in order that he might persuade his people to make these changes. He also asked for architects to be sent to build him a stone church which he promised to dedicate to St Peter. This was in effect a programme for the abandonment of the Irish Columban Church and the establishment of a truly national Pictish church. Iona with its veneration for St Columba was no longer to control the church in Pictland. In its stead was to be Nechton's stone church in the heart of the kingdom, dedicated to St Peter.

Ceolfrith sent a long letter, drafted for him by Bede, and also the architects, whose work may perhaps be seen in the curious narrow door at the base of the tower of Restenneth Priory in Angus. Bede, like Adomnan before him for the sixth century, describes the Pictish king's court in the eighth century, when the letter arrived. The Picts have come a long way. The king is no longer surrounded by pagan priests, but by learned men hard at work translating the letter. Nechton is at the centre of it all giving orders that the new Easter Tables be transcribed throughout his kingdom, contrasting with the apparent lack of interest in Columba's doings shown by Bridei. It is not known whether Bridei even agreed to be baptised himself and he appears to have made no move to grant Columba a piece of land near the royal residence on which to build a monastery.

Nechton's initiative seems to have placed the Pictish church under direct royal authority. Towards the end of the ninth century it is recorded that the reigning Scottish king was the 'first to give liberty to the Scottish Church, which was in servitude up to that time after the custom and fashion of the Picts'. Some kind of taxation imposed by the civil authorities is presumably implied by this interesting note.

For the rest of the century the Picts more than held their own politically. A leader, Oengus, son of Fergus, emerged, whose steady rise to power can be followed in entries in the Irish annals. In 741 he 'utterly destroyed' the Scots and had his ambitions stopped there we might all be living in Pictland today. But he wanted to master the Britons also, and when he failed to do so he lost Dalriada as well.

Since the origins of the Picts are obscure it is a pity that they disappear from the pages of history in a rather mysterious way. In the early medieval period kingdoms were always being lost and won, often as a result of a single victory, but that the Picts failed to recover their position when the Scots defeated them in the mid-ninth century requires explanation. There is in fact little doubt that this lies in the introduction of a new element in northern politics – the arrival of the Norse. Not very long after Oengus's death Norse raiding had begun on the northern and western coasts. As time passed, both Picts and Scots were seriously weakened fighting against them, and the Scots position on the west coast must soon have become intolerable. As soon, therefore, as they snatched a relatively minor victory over the Picts, who were by this time losing large tracts of territory in the far north, the Scots moved bodily into eastern Scotland, well away from the Norse encroachments. This was something quite different from the Northumbrian occupation of southern Pictland. The whole administration moved east, establishing itself perhaps at Forteviot where, eventually, Kenneth mac Alpin, the first king of the new kingdom of Picts and Scots, died. Kenneth also transported the relics of Columba into Pictland and built a church at Dunkeld to hold them which for a time became the chief church in the kingdom.

This is really a hypothetical solution to the way in which the Scots swamped the Picts, but it accounts for their political extinction for it would have exterminated the administration if not the population. It also accounts for the ease with which the Norse established their settlements on the west coast. A movement of the Scottish population into eastern Pictland at this period also fits well with a recent interpretation of the characteristic Pictish place-names that begin with the element *Pit-*. The second element in these names is always Irish and their formation has been dated to the period after the end of the Pictish kingdom when the two peoples were living side by side in peaceful co-existence, and Professor Jackson suggests that the incoming Irish overlords adopted the Pictish land-holding system with its 'manors' (petta) intact.

After the end of the political kingdom the Picts drop out of the records with astonishing rapidity. As a political concept they ceased to exist. The only use that medieval chroniclers found for their written sources was to use the list of the Pictish kings to extend the antiquity of the Scottish line by tacking it on behind their own king-list.

It is a notorious fact that Pictish history has to be pieced together from Irish, English and British sources and the lack of surviving Pictish sources has inevitably raised doubts as to whether in fact they had any, apart from the king-list – the most primitive of all historical records. It is true that the hold maintained by the Columban church on Pictish monasteries may have inhibited the development of written Pictish learning, particularly since initially the Irish monks may have provided a strictly classical education in their monastic schools. It is also possible that the Pictish languages may never have become fully developed written languages. After the establishment of the Pictish church, however, things must have been very different. It seems very unlikely that Nechton was unappreciative of the value of the written record and that efforts would not have been made to write down native law codes and the like. A number of reasons for the lack of surviving sources can be offered but by far the most important one must be that as the Pictish language and Pictish institutions became obsolete there would be no reason to preserve or transcribe either their Latin or vernacular sources. That the Picts participated fully in the intellectual life of the time is shown most clearly in their monumental art. The evidence it provides is full and clear and Pictish art affords a unique opportunity to comprehend something of the nature of the sensibility of the Picts. There is no Pictish saga cycle, no religious lyric poetry and no great Pictish epic but the stone sculpture compensates for these sad deficiencies to a remarkable degree.

Pictish art as we know it was in its beginnings entirely functional. By incising a series of designs on the flat surfaces of free-standing

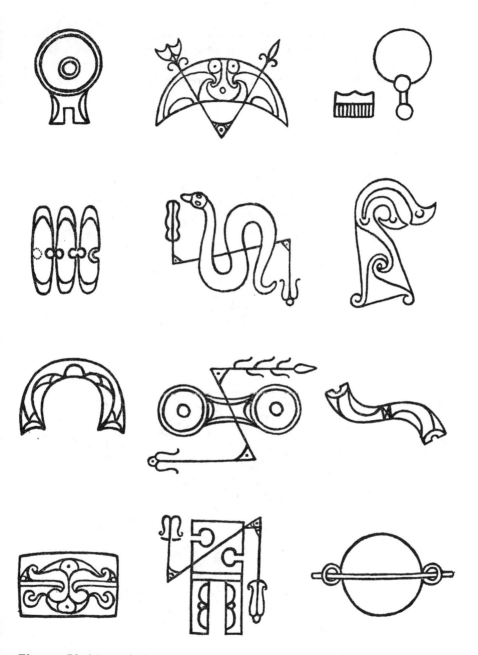

Fig 10   Pictish symbols

boulders the artists were principally engaged in conveying a message to those who looked at them. These designs are repeated in virtually identical forms all over the Pictish area and it is generally agreed that they must, therefore, be symbolic. The distribution of the symbol-bearing stones covers all the territories which

Fig 11   Pictish animal symbols

we know from the written sources to have been Pictish – from the Shetlands in the north, to Pabbay in the west, the North Sea in the east, and the Forth-Clyde line in the south. It should be noted that symbol stones are found in the districts where there were brochs, in the far north and in the Hebrides, and that these areas must not be thought of as somehow less Pictish than the eastern districts. The fact that symbol stones were erected all over Pictland suggests that this was a late custom and the lack of symbol stones in Argyll bears this out. When the Scots won this district from the Picts symbol stones were not being erected, so that they must be dated to some period after the fifth century.

The symbols, which comprise abstract designs, animal designs and a few representations of objects, are stylistically very uniform. The curvilinear patterns and the stylisation of the animals have a consistency which almost suggests that they were designed at one point in time by one school of artists. The designs are very beautiful, and the incision on the stones is even and controlled. Some of the most aesthetically successful symbols are found in the north and this could be interpreted as having a bearing on the place of origin of the designs or simply be taken as evidence for a particularly talented group of sculptors practising there. It has been suggested by Professor Charles Thomas that the stones are headstones, and that the symbols are the ancient tattoo designs, which he further believes indicated the personal rank of the tattooed individual. I have put forward a case for their being connected with ownership. In fact it is unlikely that the meaning of the symbols will ever be determined with certainty.

At a later period the symbols were used in conjunction with the cross. These monuments are properly dressed slabs with the sculptures first in very shallow relief which then gets heavier as the series progresses. An interlace cross is on the front of the slab and the symbols are usually, but not always, placed on the back. The remaining space is filled with all sorts of apparently random iconography such as hunting scenes, fantastic animals, classical motifs, and other unidentifiable figure scenes. Some of this iconography must come from portable ivories and textiles but some of it could well be illustrations of Pictish folk-tale.

Many of the features of the decoration of these cross-slabs can be paralleled in the great contemporary illuminated Gospel books of Durrow, Lindisfarne and Kells, and this provides a date of some time in the second half of the seventh century for their commencement.

Some writers have felt that many of the features of the designs on the earlier incised monuments also find their most natural analogies in these manuscripts and that some of them must therefore be as late as the seventh century. On the basis of the closeness of the resemblance in treatment of the Pictish animal designs and some of the animal evangelist symbols in three contemporary manuscripts, one of which is the Book of Durrow, I have suggested that the illuminators, seeking around for integrated animal designs for their animal symbols, lighted upon the already existing powerful Pictish animal designs. If this is so, then the symbol stones pre-date or are at least contemporary with the earliest of these Hiberno-Saxon manuscripts. Professor Thomas would release the early symbol stones entirely from their connections with the manuscript tradition and dates them even earlier. These matters cannot be discussed here but what should be emphasised is the extremely high quality of Pictish sculpture. The Picts were obviously naturally talented artists with a highly developed sense of line and composition. From the start they had no difficulty in laying out interlace designs and later they exploited brilliantly the resources of relief sculpture. Their repertoire, while clearly related to what was going on in England and Ireland, remained individual. Their interest in David iconography is so marked as to suggest the existence in Pictland of an illustrated Psalter. Their fondness for spiral designs of great complexity is not found in other contemporary stone sculpture. The nature of the cross-slab, itself a peculiarity of the Picts, allowed them space to produce an extended piece of secular narrative art such as the battle-scene in Aberlemno churchyard which is unparalleled. On the other hand the magnificent cross slab from Nigg, aswirl with curves and bosses is aesthetically very close indeed to the well-known Chi-Rho page in the Book of Kells. The figure sculpture on this slab also recalls the figure style of the Kells school.

The great monuments of Nigg, Hilton of Cadboll and the sarcophagus at St Andrews represent some of the most impressive monuments of the latest phase of Pictish sculpture. The sarcophagus bears no symbols but its David iconography and its enmeshed bosses surrounded by snakes link it firmly with a symbol-bearing monument such as Nigg. Many splendid crosses of this period, particularly in the north, survive in fragments only. Tarbat in Ross appears to have had a number of them and must have been a very important centre. A fragment, now in Elgin museum, of a figure of David virtually identical with the figure on the sarcophagus, is all that is left of what must have been a sculpture of comparable distinction. These crosses were clearly raised in considerable numbers by artists of superlative capacity for patrons of sensibility and taste and in themselves provide irrefutable evidence for the intellectual awareness of Pictish society.

The Picts, then, have left perhaps their most distinctive mark on Scotland in their sculptured stones scattered over the countryside. Did they contribute any other lasting effect on the later kingdom of Scotland? Pictish families, particularly in the north-east, may have persisted for many years after the Scots took over, and local methods of administration and land-tenure are unlikely to have been instantly uprooted. A close scrutiny of the sources for medieval Scottish history may reveal traces of this kind of Pictish continuity. At present, however, it can only be said, in sentimental vein, that if we Scots like to think of ourselves as something distinct from an Irish colony then it is the spirit of the tribes who went to make up the Picts that we must invoke.

CHAPTER V

The Scots of Dalriada

John Bannerman

'No Scot ever set his foot on British soil save from a vessel that had put out from Ireland.' Latin writers of the early centuries of our era, whether continental or insular, refer to the inhabitants of Ireland as *Scotti* or Scots and to Ireland itself as *Scotia*. They spoke Gaelic, a Celtic language, which is a continuing part of our heritage, and Gaelic culture is increasingly recognised to have been an important factor in the preservation of our identity as a people. The term for a Scot in his own language was *Gàidheal* or Gael, although today it describes a Gaelic-speaking Scot only.

Population movements in Ireland in the fourth and fifth centuries resulted in settlements of Scotti along the western sea-board of the neighbouring island of Britain. In Scotland itself, the penetration was even greater. We find Scotti, apparently acting in conjunction with the Picts, harassing the Roman province of Britain in the vicinity of the Walls in the fourth century, and this should probably be seen in the context of traditional material, supported by place-name study, which tells of early settlements of Scotti, apparently from Munster, in the Pictish province of Circinn, now Angus and the Mearns, in the Lennox district of the British kingdom of Strathclyde, and elsewhere.

But the history of the Scots in Scotland begins with the foundation of the kingdom of Dalriada, mainly Argyll and its islands, in what was presumably once part of Pictland. It is not clear when the Scots of Dalriada in Ireland, which corresponded more or less to the present day coastal area of County Antrim, began to cross the narrow stretch of intervening sea, but when their royal dynasty, in the person of Fergus Mór, son of Erc, forsook Dunseverick, their Irish capital, and took up permanent residence in Scotland around A.D. 500, it can fairly be assumed that their overseas colony was not only securely established but already overtaking in importance the mother country. It is arguable that the advent of Fergus Mór is the single most important event in Scotland's history. To this we owe two basic facts of life, that we are today Scots living in a country called Scotland. From Fergus Mór, with a few early exceptions, descend all subsequent kings and queens of Scots, including the present Queen of Great Britain; pride in the antiquity of the dynasty was to be a unifying factor at periods of crisis in our later history.

An event of almost equal significance was the advent of yet another Scot from Ireland in 563, namely Columba, or, to give him his Gaelic name, *Colum Cille*, 'Dove of the Church'. He was a scion of the royal family of the Uí Néill, the most powerful people in Ireland of the time. He was to become the paramount saint of the Scots. And although the Scots, in their attempts, culminating in the *Declaration of Arbroath* of 1320, to persuade the papal authorities that their church and state were independent of England, claimed the Apostle Andrew, brother of St Peter of Rome, as their patron saint, it was the *Brecbennach* of Columba, housed at Arbroath, then the premier monastery in Scotland, which protected the Scots at Bannockburn. Indeed, if the Scot today was asked to name the most spiritually significant centre in his country, invariably his answer would be Iona, the small island off the west coast of Mull on which Columba founded his monastery.

The period during which Fergus Mór flourished may be calculated from the extant Irish annals, which incorporate a chronicle apparently compiled in Iona in the first half of the eighth century. The fullest versions are contained in the *Annals of Ulster* and the *Annals of Tigernach*. It is the most informative source for the early political history of Dalriada. Adomnan, abbot of Iona (d. 704), who wrote a life of Columba within a century of the latter's death in 597, was primarily concerned to prove the sanctity of Columba, but he has much to tell us not only of the saint's life and career but also of the history of Dalriada in his own time and earlier. The work is also a valuable commentary on the social and economic life of the area. The *Senchus Fer nAlban*, 'History of the Men of Scotland', a seventh century compilation in origin, records the genealogies of the ruling families in Dalriada and is also in some degree a census of the military and economic resources of its people. The early eighth century *Genelaig Albanensium*, 'Scottish Pedigrees', seems to be a continuation of the genealogical section of the *Senchus*. Finally, chronicles, which consist mainly of lists of kings of Scots with the lengths of their reigns, are extant from the eleventh century. The most important non-native source is Bede's *Ecclesiastical History of the English*

People, completed in 731. Bede, a Northumbrian monk, was particularly interested in the church which emanated from Iona and which played such a large part in bringing Christianity to the Angles of Northumbria. However, although it is true to say that the Scots of Dalriada are the most fully documented of all the Dark Age peoples in what is now Scotland, there are and will continue to be many gaps in our knowledge of their history.

All the sources listed above mention Aedán, great-grandson of Fergus Mór, and king of Dalriada from 574 to about 608. He is easily the most considerable lay figure among the Scots until Kenneth, son of Alpin, in whose reign the political union of Scots and Picts was effected in 843–4. To some extent, one can judge this by the amount of information extant concerning his career. There are records of battles fought by him in the Isle of Man, in Ireland, in the Orkneys, in the Pictish province of Circinn, and against the Maeatae of central Scotland. The only real setback of his career was a defeat inflicted on him by the Angles of Northumbria at the unidentified Degsastán in 603. But the point to note here is that this battle was fought on Northumbrian soil.

Aedán's extension of the power and prestige of the Scots owed much to the support and counsel which he received from Columba. Columba's most significant act in this context was to win the friendship of, and apparently convert to Christianity, Bridei (Brude), over-king of all the Picts (d. 584), especially as Bridei had already inflicted a defeat on the Scots some sixteen years before Aedán's succession. Iona, Bede tells us, 'held for a long time pre-eminence over the monasteries of all the Picts, and was their superior in ruling their communities'. According to Adomnan, Columba consecrated Aedán king of Dalriada on Iona, the earliest documentary reference to a ceremony of ordination of a king of Scots in Scotland. We find him advising Aedán at the Convention of Druim Cett in 575 in the latter's dialogue with Aed, son of Ainmire, king of the Uí Néill, concerning the future status of Aedán's Irish territories. He is recorded as praying for Aedán's success in battle with the Maeatae, while Aedán is seen taking his advice as to which of his sons should succeed him as king of Scots. The importance of this partnership between church and state, demonstrated so clearly in Aedán's reign, cannot be over-estimated, it is a recurring theme which extends far beyond the period of Dalriada's existence as a separate entity.

In the *Senchus Fer nAlban*, three chief peoples are named in seventh century Dalriada. The least important of these was the Cenél nOengusa, 'kindred of Oengus', who inhabited the island of Islay. The Cenél nGabráin, 'kindred of Gabrán', named for Aedán's father, occupied Kintyre, with Gigha, possibly also Jura, and Crích Chomgaill, 'the territory of Comgall', present day Cowal, with its islands, certainly Bute, but probably Arran also. The Cenél Loairn, 'kindred of Loarn', occupied the territory so-called today and the island of Colonsay, and, by implication, dominated all the islands and mainland districts to the north of these not inhabited by the Picts. On the mainland, the boundary between them probably ran somewhere to the north of Ardnamurchan, while Columba is said to have baptised a Pict on the island of Skye. To the east, the ridge of mountains known in Gaelic as Druim Alban separated Scot from Pict. The strongholds of the Cenél nGabráin, at least around 700, were Dunaverty in the Mull of Kintyre and Tairpert Boitter, presumably near Tarbert, Lochfyne, while Dunollie, near Oban, and Dunadd on the Crinan Canal were the contemporary strongholds of the Cenél Loairn.

As the names of these peoples suggest, the structure of society was kin-based. The basic kin group was the *derbfine* or 'certain kin', which consisted of four generations of descendants including the common ancestor, that is to say, an ancestor, his sons, grandsons, and great-grandsons. It was with the *derbfine* that responsibility for liabilities incurred by any one of its members lay, and all members of this group were heirs in respect of property, personal and landed. The ruler of each of the kindreds named above was a *rí* or king, with the king of the Cenél nGabráin overlord of Dalriada at this time. Succession to the kingship was decided within the *derbfine* of a king. A study of the application and occurence in the Irish annals of the term *rígdomnae*, literally, 'material of a king', that is, a person eligible to succeed to the kingship, shows that dynastic succession lay with members of the *derbfine*, the common ancestor of which had himself been a king. In the hope, often deferred, of avoiding internal strife among what would normally be a large number of eligible males within the royal kindred, a successor was appointed during the lifetime of the reigning king. He was called *tánaise ríg*, 'second to a king', from which derive the English terms for the system *tanistry* and *tanist*. The intention was to secure the person best fitted for the job. He was to be of

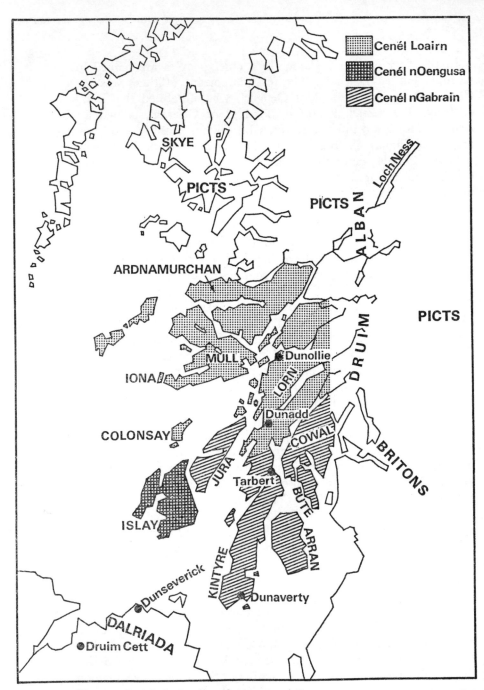

Cenél Loairn
Cenél nOengusa
Cenél nGabrain

SKYE

PICTS

PICTS

ALBAN

Loch Ness

ARDNAMURCHAN

PICTS

MULL

Dunollie

IONA

LORN

DRUIM

COLONSAY

Dunadd

COWAL

BRITONS

JURA

Tarbert

BUTE

ISLAY

ARRAN

KINTYRE

Dunseverick

Dunaverty

DALRIADA

Druim Cett

Fig 12   Dalriada in the 7th century A.D.

age and sound in mind and body. It was therefore unusual for a son or grandson to succeed, although perfectly legal given the right circumstances, while the succession of a brother, a nephew, or a cousin was more likely. This pattern of succession to the kingship of the Scots, with the later innovation, probably Pictish in origin, that it could pass through a female, was to obtain without interruption into the twelfth century and remained a factor in the succession stakes for some centuries thereafter.

The other free grades in lay society were the noble and the commoner. The noble was generally a close relative of the contemporary king or a descendant of relatives of earlier kings. All commoners were in a client relationship to the nobles and, as far as the *Senchus* was concerned, were expressed in terms of houses. Thus, the Cenél nGabráin had 560 houses or clients, while the Cenél Loairn and the Cenél nOengusa had 420 and 430 respectively.

From every twenty houses were to come two seven-benched boats, which probably meant that every twenty houses was to provide twenty-eight oarsmen, allowing for two to a bench as would be normal. The necessity for such a system of recruitment is testimony to the importance of naval power to the sea-girt inhabitants of Dalriada, already exemplified in the military expeditions undertaken by Aedán involving long sea voyages. The Gaelic *curach* was a word frequently used to describe the vessels which plied Dalriadic waters at this time; their lineal descendants, still so described, are in use today along the west coast of Ireland. Structurally, the *curach* consisted of a framework of wood covered with pitched hides, now tarred calico. In addition to oars, it had a sail. According to Adomnan, it was a ship of this kind which sailed northwards for fourteen days and nights, 'beyond the range of human exploration', before returning. The twenty house unit of Dalriada has echoes in the fiscal organisation of later medieval Scotland.

The *Senchus* also allows us to estimate in round figures the number of men which each kindred could muster for a *slógad* or hosting, 800 from the Cenél nGabráin, 700 from the Cenél Loairn, and from the Cenél nOengusa 500. Thus, Aedán's armies, in so far as they were drawn from Dalriada in Scotland, cannot have numbered more than 2,000 men at any one time, although we do know that he had a contingent direct from Ireland at the battle of Degsastán. One hundred of the seven hundred men which the Cenél Loairn could muster were Airgialla, the name for a group of peoples in a vassal relationship to the Uí Néill in Northern Ireland. It seems that they were of the Northern Uí Macc-Uais, a section of which had apparently settled in the islands dominated by the Cenél Loairn and were performing military service for the latter, a function which this people had already carried out for the Uí Néill in Ireland.

In conclusion, what strikes one most forcibly when examining in detail the system of society obtaining among the Scots of Dalriada and in contemporary Ireland is how often its constituent elements find their precise equivalent in the so-called clan system of later Scotland.

The culture of the Scots of Dalriada, as might be expected, mirrors that of contemporary Ireland. And indeed, Gaelic-speaking Scotland and Ireland constituted a single culture-province down into the seventeenth century. The obituary notices of famous people, especially of the professional and ecclesiastical classes, often represent them as being equally well-known in Ireland and Scotland. Thus, in the *Annals of Tigernach*, Mael-dúin, bishop of the Scots (d. 1055), resident in the monastic community at St Andrews, is eulogised as 'the glory of the Gaels', that is, of the inhabitants of Scotland and Ireland.

The church in Ireland, and therefore in Dalriada, neither of which was ever part of the Roman Empire, was not imposed by conquerors but was truly missionary in character, recruiting from the beginning most of its members on the spot. And after some initial hostility, the most fertile ground for recruitment was the existing native learned classes. The result was a fusion of Christian and Mediterranean cultural influences with pagan and vernacular learning. The whole process received an even greater impetus, when, by the sixth century, the church had become predominantly monastic in character, a type of monasticism, moreover, at once ascetic and intellectual, promoting through the monastic school the education of laymen. It has been estimated that, by the eighth century, the proportion of literate laymen in the areas served by the Celtic church must have been abnormally high when compared with the rest of Northern Europe. It is significant that one of the earliest and most important extant poems in the vernacular is an elegy to Columba, the greatest of the educated religious of the Celtic church, probably composed around 600 by Dallán Forgaill, a lay poet said to be the most renowned of his time in

1   Ring of Brodgar, Orkney

2   Broch of Mousa, Shetland

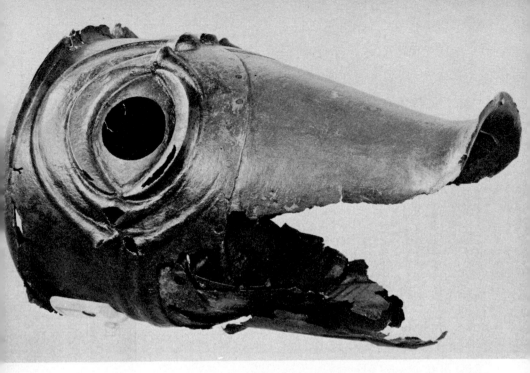

3 Celtic bronze trumpet, Deskford, Banffshire

4 Roman distance-slab, Hutcheson Hill, Glasgow

5 Pictish symbol stones: (left) Glamis Manse (right) Aberlemno Churchyard

6 Dumbarton Rock

7 Iona Abbey (and St Martin's Cross)

8 Monymusk Reliquary (Brecbennach of
St Columba)

9 Ruthwell Cross, Dumfriesshire

10   Kildalton Cross, Islay   11   Anglian panel (detail) from Jedburgh Abbey

12   Mote of Urr, Kirkcudbrightshire

13   Part of Norse settlement, Jarlshof, Shetland

14   Viking hoard, Skaill, Orkney

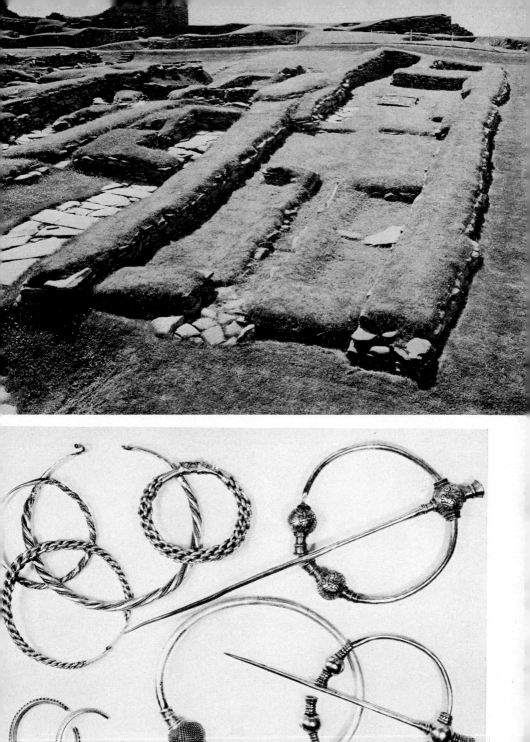

15   Norman church, Leuchars, Fife

16   Dirleton Castle, East Lothian

Ireland. But more than that, Columba himself was, according to early tradition, a poet of note in the vernacular, and he was certainly a Latin scribe; Adomnan portrays him on the very day of his death in the process of copying a psalter.

But monastic scribes did not confine themselves to the mechanical process of copying the scriptures, they began to make original contributions to ecclesiastical literature, the most characteristic being saints' lives. One of the earliest and most interesting was the *Life of Columba* by Adomnan. Adomnan also wrote an account of the holy places in the Eastern Mediterranean from notes dictated to him by a bishop of Gaul who had travelled in the area and whom Adomnan had entertained on Iona for a time. His writings indicate a library at Iona of considerable resources, containing, among other things, works of Jerome and of Sulpicius Severus, Pope Gregory I's *Dialogues,* Athanasius's *Life of St Anthony,* Hegesippus, alongside Solinus and Virgil's *Aeneid* of pre-Christian antiquity, but the influence of the vernacular tradition is also evident, many of his stories demonstrating Columba's miraculous powers are based upon the oral literature of the time. And it was not long before the monastic scribes were recording in writing the native tradition as it stood. The result is that we have in Gaelic the oldest vernacular literature in Western Europe.

The single most important body of early vernacular literature preserved for us by the labours of the Celtic church monks were the sagas, particularly the Ulster Cycle with Cú Chulainn as its central figure; and also the cycle of sagas associated with Fionn and his son Ossian whose names, by the nineteenth century, had become familiar far beyond the bounds of Scotland and Ireland. The typical product of the lay poet of the period was praise poetry, eulogy and elegy, aimed at the elevation of kindreds and the heads of kindreds. Even here the influence of the church is evident, for the metres were modelled on early continental Latin hymn metres, and they continued in use in Scotland into the eighteenth century. But more than that, the subject matter was considerably widened and includes what we would now call nature poetry, an extraordinary manifestation centuries before it appears in the literature of other peoples.

Deriving directly from the scriptoria of the Celtic church monasteries is the school of manuscript illumination, which has been described as 'the finest flower of Celtic art'. The traditional curvilinear treatment of ornament, incorporating fantastic animal figures and spiralling foliage, either present for its own sake or as a frame for representations of scriptural motifs, is generally thought to have reached its peak with the *Book of Kells*, a large Gospel book intended to lie on the altar. Begun, it seems, in the Iona scriptorium around 800, it was described by the *Annals of Ulster* in 1007 as 'the chief relic of the Western World'.

The style and artistry of the illuminated manuscript was reproduced on contemporary stone-work, sometimes so exactly as to imply direct influence of one on the other. Thus, the great wheeled crosses of St Martin and St John on Iona have on them representations of the Virgin and Child surrounded by angels found elsewhere only in a page of the *Book of Kells*. The bosses standing out in high relief, which are so characteristic a feature of these crosses and, more particularly, of the cross at Kildalton in Islay, remind us of metalwork, an art in which the Celts, whether in their continental or insular setting, are generally recognised to have excelled. The Hunterston Brooch, which dates to the early eighth century, has few rivals for excellence in workmanship and is a fine example of the Celtic artist's propensity for making the most of a limited space with complex and detailed but perfectly proportioned ornament. Although found at Hunterston, Ayrshire, it is probably of Dalriadic origin. Nor should we forget, since we have already had occasion to mention it, the reliquary from Monymusk of the same period, which is in the form of a house-shrine made of wood, elaborately decorated with metalwork, and almost certainly the *Brecbennach* of Columba.

A surface crowded with stylised representation and ornament, at its best so delicately proportioned and imaginatively varied in treatment as to defeat totally the onset of monotony, and the love of clear and distinct colour are perhaps the most characteristic features of the visual arts. But they are also present in literature, particularly in poetry, notable for the variety of literary ornament and metre. It is not unlikely that the music of the harp, for long the most highly regarded instrument among the Scots, if it had survived, would have exhibited the same love of decorative variation. It is certainly present in the classical music of the bagpipe, which had overtaken the harp in popularity by the seventeenth century. These are the factors which give the culture of the Scots in all its aspects a notable unity of form and purpose.

The political fortunes of the Scots of Dalriada took a backward step in the reign of Domnall Brecc, Aedán's grandson. It is recorded that he was defeated in battle on no less than four occasions. His opponents may have been Picts in 634 and 638 but, in 637, his participation in the well-known battle of Magh Rath in Co. Down against Domnall, son of Aed, king of the Uí Néill, seems to have cost him his Irish territories. Dalriada in Ireland was no longer to be ruled from Scotland. At Strathcarron about 642, Domnall Brecc met his death at the hands of the Britons of Strathclyde; a famous victory this and a stanza commemorating it, incorporated in the British poem *Gododdin*, ends with the words 'and the head of Domnall Brecc, ravens gnawed it'. This is the earliest certain record of hostility between Scot and Briton in Scotland.

Internally, the chief result of Domnall Brecc's disastrous career seems to have been to weaken the Cenél nGabráin, allowing the Cenél Loairn to move into the ascendancy towards the end of the century and Ferchar Fota (d. 697) was the first of their leaders to figure in the list of the kings of Dalriada. It seems also to have promoted a split in the Cenél nGabráin itself. The Cenél Comgaill, who inhabited Crích Chomgaill or Cowal and who were named for Comgall, Gabrán's brother and predecessor as king of Dalriada, had taken their place alongside the other three peoples of Dalriada by 700.

The Cenél Loairn's period of dominance was anything but a peaceful one for them. Internal troubles resulted in Selbach, their leader and king of Dalriada, destroying Dunollie, one of their own strongholds, in 701. Thirteen years later, he rebuilt it. Nor did the Cenél nGabráin allow the Cenél Loairn to hold undisputed sway over Dalriada, and although the latter normally held them off successfully, they defeated Selbach in a *bellum maritimum* in 719, the first sea-battle recorded in the history of the British Isles. Finally, as the leading people of Dalriada at this time, the Cenél Loairn had to bear the brunt of what seems to have been the first and last sustained campaign against the Scots by the neighbouring Picts under their king Oengus. This Pictish aggression culminated in 741 with 'the smiting of Dalriada by Oengus, son of Fergus'.

It has generally been thought that Dalriada remained under the heel of Pictland until the political union of the two countries about 843 and consequently it has been usual to express surprise that the union was effected by the king of Scots rather than a king of the numerically superior Picts. True there was no further reference to Dalriada in a political context until 768. But this was a battle between Picts and Scots in Fortriu, now Strathearn and Menteith, a Pictish province neighbouring on Dalriada. It seems that the prevailing pattern of aggression by the Scots at the expense of the Picts had already reasserted itself. The king of Scots involved was Aed Find of the Cenél nGabráin, and it may be taken that one result of the Pictish invasion of Dalriada was the elimination of the Cenél Loairn as a contender for political leadership in the country. Thereafter, Fortriu and Dalriada are closely connected, with kings of Dalriada who were sometimes also recorded as kings of Fortriu.

At the outset, this makes it less surprising that Kenneth, son of Alpin, of the Cenél nGabráin (d. 858), should have brought Scots and Picts together in a lasting political union. It has, however, been suggested that Kenneth may have had a valid claim to succeed to the kingship of the Picts in the female line. Other sources assert that the union was the result of military conquest by Kenneth, possibly aided by reinforcement direct from Ireland, and perhaps only after the Picts had been weakened by a defeat at the hands of a marauding Danish army. And indeed, there are frequent references to Scandinavian raids on both Dalriada and Pictland from the beginning of this century, so that a drawing together in the face of a common enemy is a not unlikely trend.

A combination of some or all of these factors would explain why the union took place when it did, but it does not explain the virtual disappearance of the Picts from history, a disappearance so complete that certain twelfth century English chroniclers were able to make the extraordinary error of locating Picts in Galloway. The most likely explanation is that the Scoticisation of the Picts was well under way by the time of the union, which is in itself, of course, a fundamental reason for the union taking place under a king of Scots. Settlements of Scots in parts of Pictland, beginning, it seems, at least as early as the fourth century, must have played their part in the process but the most important factor was surely the introduction of Christianity to the Picts by the Scots. The linguistic and cultural penetration of Pictland following in its wake cannot be over-estimated. The new kingdom of the Scots became known as *Alba* in Gaelic and *Scotia* in Latin, names which are, of course, current today.

Just as did Fergus Mór three and a half centuries earlier, the kings of Scots went east, enabling them to take a firmer grip of their vastly extended territories. Their southern boundary was now the Forth-Clyde line. They took up residence at Scone, which became the *caput* or legal centre of Scotland. Centuries later, in his bid for the kingship of the Scots, Robert Bruce was careful to have himself crowned at Scone, but, because Edward I of England had already removed it to Westminster, could not be installed on the coronation stone of the king of Scots, generally known as the Stone of Destiny, which, tradition has it, was brought by the Scots from Ireland, first to Iona and then, presumably after the union, to Scone.

The kings of Scotia were of the Cenél nGabráin, but the ruling family of their erstwhile rivals the Cenél Loairn also seem to have shared in the eastward expansion. Thus, an eleventh century mormaer (later *comes* or earl) of Moray derived his descent from Ferchar Fota of the Cenél Loairn. As the Cenél nGabráin expanded through the Perthshire glens linking Dalriada with Pictland, so the obvious and perhaps the only conceivable outlet to the east for the Cenél Loairn, situated as they were in Northern Dalriada, was up the Great Glen and into Moray. The later aspirations of the Men of Moray to elevate members of their ruling family into the kingship of the Scots, successful in the case of Macbeth (d. 1057) and of his successor Lulach (d. 1058), although both also had legitimate claims to succeed within the kin-based system of succession, may well have been inspired by the memory that the Cenél Loairn once competed with the Cenél nGabráin in the provision of kings of Dalriada.

The vacuum which may have been created in Dalriada as a result of the removal of the ruling families of the Cenél nGabráin and the Cenél Loairn seems to have been filled by the Airgialla, the people whom we saw subordinated to the Cenél Loairn in the seventh and early eighth centuries. It would be natural for them to increase in power and influence as the Cenél Loairn was weakened by internal strife and Pictish aggression in the first half of the eighth century. Whatever the case, Gofraid, son of Fergus, apparently a member of their ruling family, came over from Ireland with an army to assist Kenneth, son of Alpin, and settled in the islands. His descendants, at first submerged under Norse overlordship in the area, were to re-emerge in the twelfth century in the person of Somerled, 'king of the Isles' (d. 1164), who was, in turn, ancestor of the later Lords of the Isles.

In keeping with the partnership between church and state so evident in the time of Columba and Aedán, the administrative centre of the church moved east with Kenneth. Thus, in 849, a division of the relics of Columba seems to have been made, some going to the monastery of Dunkeld and some to the monastery of Kells in Northern Ireland. In the Celtic church, the authority of the founding saint went with his relics and the result was to split the Columban church in two. The reason for the removal of some of Columba's relics to Kells, which now became head of all the Columban monasteries in Northern Ireland, was the increasingly insistent presence in the waters between Ireland and Scotland of Norse sea-going raiders whose first attack on Iona had come towards the end of the previous century. This does not mean that Iona was abandoned. A monastic community continued in existence there. Iona itself remained the spiritual centre of the church and almost all the kings of Scots down to Domnall Bán, whose reign ended in 1097, are said to have been buried there.

A further shift of the administrative centre of the church from Dunkeld to St Andrews had almost certainly been accomplished by 943 when Constantine II, king of Scots, abdicated to become abbot of the Culdee monastery at St Andrews, and there it remained until the Reformation. No doubt the relics of Columba went too – this would explain how the *Brecbennach* came in time to be housed in the monastery of Arbroath, also on the east coast. But the fact that the monastic community at St Andrews belonged to the Culdee order is itself sufficient indication of the presence of the Columban church. The Culdees, that is, *Céli Dé*, 'Clients of God', came into being as the result of a reform movement within the church in Ireland in the second half of the eighth century. Perhaps because there was a community of Culdees at Iona, as well as at St Andrews, the order seems to have been particularly strong in Scotland and their monasteries also included Abernethy, Brechin, Loch Leven, Monifieth, Monymusk and Muthil. At the first two of these are located the best preserved examples of round towers in Scotland, again typical of the church in Ireland, where the earliest seem to date to the tenth century. They were built partly as bell towers but also for defence, particularly for the protection of the precious relics of the monastery.

A constant factor in the history of the Scots from the period of migration from Ireland right through to the twelfth century was their urge to expand into new territories. Immediately the union of Scots and Picts was effected, they turned their eyes southwards and Kenneth himself, we are told, undertook no less than six invasions of Lothian, still the northern part of the kingdom of Northumbria. In Indulf's reign (954–62), the Scots captured the stronghold of Edinburgh and, in 1018, Malcolm II won the battle of Carham which finally secured possession of Lothian for the Scots. About this time, and, presumably through a dynastic connection, Duncan, Malcolm II's grandson, succeeded to the British kingdom of Strathclyde. So that when Duncan became king of Scots on his grandfather's death in 1034, the bounds of Scotland were fixed more or less as they are today, although the border, as we know it, had still to be precisely defined.

The story of the continued expansion of the Scots can be read on the ground, as it were, in the spread of Gaelic place-names over the country. For the Picts, partly a Celtic speaking people, the transition to Gaelic cannot have been too difficult. Nor yet for the Britons of Strathclyde, and here we should not forget an earlier and independent movement, beginning in the early tenth century, into Galloway and Carrick, perhaps from the Western Isles, perhaps from Ireland, of a people who, although of mixed Scotto-Norse origin, were already largely Gaelic speaking. But the evidence of place and personal names shows that even Lothian must have had a considerable Gaelic-speaking aristocracy by the twelfth century.

The Scoticisation of almost the whole of what we have come to know as Scotland by the opening of the twelfth century cannot be too strongly stressed. It survived the influx in this century of people and ideas which flowed from the Norman Conquest of England. Thus, in the fourteenth century, Robert Bruce, king of Scots but bearer of an Anglo-Norman name, was able to urge the Irish to join with the Scots and rise against English domination, reminding them that the Scots and Irish shared a common origin, common customs and a common language.

CHAPTER VI

Britons and Angles
D. P. Kirby

What can be termed the Forth-Tyne or Clyde-Solway province of
Dark Age Britain formed the originally British (P-Celtic) territory
of what was to become in large measure part of Scotland. Though
the population may have been basically of non-Celtic prehistoric
origin at the time of the Roman Conquest, Celtic Brythonic
chieftains were probably in the ascendancy. By the early fifth
century, at the end of the Roman period, older British folk-groups
– the Damnonii across the valley of the Clyde, the Novantae and
Selgovae of Dumfriesshire and Galloway, and the Votadini between the Tyne and the Forth – were evolving into primitive states,
possibly as specifically frontier states with the military task of
containing the attacks of Picts and Scots from the north and west.

Strathclyde, Rheged, and the kingdom of the Gododdin emerge
most clearly. The frontiers of Strathclyde reached to the '*Clach
nam Breatann*' (Stone of the Britons) on the western side of Glen
Falloch at the head of Loch Lomond in the north and nearly to
Stirling in the east. From the fifth century Dumbarton was the
capital of Strathclyde. The immediate vicinity of Stirling was
known as Manaw of the Gododdin, and Stirling and Edinburgh
were Gododdin strongholds. The heartland of Rheged appears to
have been the Eden valley, e.g. Carlisle. Traprain Law, near
Haddington, is the classic site at present from North Britain, revealing in its treasure the interaction of Roman and native and
apparently enjoying a continuous occupation into the Dark Ages.
These kingdoms were all part of a network of British states which
stretched across the whole of immediate post-Roman Britain.

In the course of the fifth and sixth centuries the Angles, Saxons
and Jutes from North Germany and Denmark overran most of
what is now England. Cornwall and the Lake District remained
British as did Wales and North Britain. The Britons put up a
fierce resistance to the Anglo-Saxons but were unable to contain
the incoming hordes. The struggle in North Britain is unusually
well documented. The North British scene can be reconstructed
from the British writings of Gildas in the sixth century and Nennius

in the early ninth, from the extant pedigrees of North British ruling families, and from the British bardic compositions of Taliesin and Aneirin which are generally believed to date to the late sixth century. It is clear that the North British area by the time of the Anglo-Saxon onslaught was at least nominally Christian. This is evident from archaeological excavations at Whithorn, for example, and, as the period progresses, Ardwall Isle, from the distribution of early inscribed Christian stones such as the famous 'Peter' stone at Whithorn or that at Yarrowkirk which commemorates two otherwise unknown princes, and from the bardic poems with their references to 'Heaven' and 'Easter'.

The Britons would be conscious that they were Christians when confronting the pagan Picts, and the missionary activities of the Whithorn-based Ninianic Church in the fifth century may have been intended to tame the enemy. But the Scots were Christians with their own priests. St Columba founded Iona in 563. For a relatively recently converted people like the Britons, as with other primitive peoples on other occasions, there must have been tremendous psychological tensions in having to resist at one and the same time both pagans and Christians. The Britons nevertheless achieved considerable success. They managed to confine the Picts and Scots above the Forth and the Clyde. It is not clear who was the dominant British leader at any one time. Coel the Old, in the early fifth century, was the progenitor of many northern dynasties including that of Rheged. Ceretic of Dumbarton, whom St Patrick reproached for his slave-raids on Ireland, and who was approximately Coel's contemporary, was the ancestor of the kings of Strathclyde. Later on Arthur must have been a leader of some significance. The Welsh annals date his death at *Camlann* to 537 and *Camlann* could be Birdoswald on Hadrian's Wall. Nennius locates one of his battles in the Caledonian forest, which, if true would place this particular campaign in the heart of Southern Pictland, and it is possible to see Arthur as one of the commanders primarily responsible for checking Pictish and Scottish advances. His alleged connection with what is now Southern England, with South Cadbury for example, or Cornwall, is much more tenuous.

In the 580s and 590s one of the principal warriors among the North Britons is said by Nennius to have been Urbgen (or Urien), lord of Rheged, in Taliesin's words 'Golden King of the North'. By this date the main antagonists to the North Britons were the

F

Angles of Northumbria. Established in Yorkshire or Deira from the fifth century, a new Anglian spearhead under Ida struck inland from Bamburgh and Lindisfarne in the mid-sixth century to establish the kingdom of Bernicia (which ultimately became part of Northumbria). It was against the successors of Ida in Bernicia that Urbgen led a great North British coalition, including Rhydderch, king of Strathclyde (afterwards remembered as the patron of St Kentigern). Urbgen was slain during a subsequent siege of the Angles on Lindisfarne by a rival British leader, Morcant, ostensibly one of his allies and perhaps a king of the Galloway area. The death of Urbgen appears to have been followed by widespread disintegration of the British kingdoms of the north. Under the attack of a succession of very able kings of Northumbria, drawn primarily from Bernicia, the major British states, with the exception of Strathclyde, collapsed. The Votadini counter-attacked only to be defeated at *Catraeth* (Catterick), a catastrophe comparable perhaps to the calamity which befell the Scots at Flodden many centuries later. The epic British poem describing the disaster at *Catraeth* is known as the *Gododdin* of Aneirin. Even Aedán, king of Dalriada, was defeated in 604 when he came to the aid of the Britons. In 638 the Northumbrians captured Edinburgh and in 642 Stirling. At the same time the Bernician royal family seems to have acquired Rheged by a diplomatic marriage. In this tremendous upheaval many Britons evidently fled south into Wales and hence the earliest Welsh literature is dominated by 'the men of the North', as they were known, and recalled the deeds of Arthur, Rhydderch and Urbgen and many others, not least Merlin. Later, in the romances of the middle Ages, Melrose, for example, became *'Mons Dolorosus'*, the homeland of Tristan was *'Loenois'* (Lothian), and Carlisle appeared as one of Arthur's great courts. The legend lingered on and, though the reality was probably grim, the magic has not yet entirely lost its spell.

With no fundamental linguistic differences and not least because of the western seaways, the Britons of Wales were able to maintain contact with the Britons of Strathclyde. A stray stanza in the *Gododdin* records the defeat and slaying in 642 of Domnall Brecc, king of Dalriada, by the Strathclyde Britons, and the Welsh annals show that events in Strathclyde might occasionally be recorded in Wales down into the early eleventh century.

Moreover, Anglian settlement across North Britain was, with

the exception of East Lothian, probably not very intensive, certainly not in the further western regions. In Galloway and Dumfriesshire the pockets of densest settlement were in the vicinities of Whithorn and Hoddom. The seventh century Northumbrian palace, with timber halls and other buildings enclosed with a palisade, at Yeavering in the Cheviots, was in the centre of a British complex. An apparently British hall, recently excavated near Dunbar, together with a subsequent Anglian hall on the same site, both with structural features related to the Yeavering buildings, suggests that the craftsmen at Yeavering drew in part on native British tradition. In this connection it is interesting that Rhun, son of Urbgen, may have worked as a missionary in the vicinity of Yeavering in the 620s. A rectangular timber hall, 55 ft. by 18 ft., of undoubted British construction and dating to the sixth or seventh centuries, has recently been excavated at Kirkconnel in Dumfriesshire. Early Anglian colonisation in the border counties was essentially in the valleys and of limited proportions. Such linear earthwork defensive constructions as the Catrail in Roxburghshire or the De'il's Dyke in Dumfriesshire and Ayrshire may have been British attempts to restrict settlement and expansion. Moreover, across most of this area there survived a rural economy and a social pattern similar if not virtually identical in kind to that in Wales and Scotland. Taxes were traditionally levied in cattle; and pastoral, semi-agricultural settlements depended for survival on summer grazings away from the house dwellings. This is a fundamental aspect of agrarian development in North Britain which has really only begun to be explored in the light of later medieval documents. The evidence would certainly indicate, however, that the Angles failed to colonise this region intensively enough to obliterate Celtic custom. Perhaps a situation again prevailed here as on the eve of the Roman Conquest in which an older population and society survived but under the dominance of a minority alien aristocracy.

The cultural development of much of North Britain under Northumbrian domination was shaped by this Anglian élite. Examples of early British monumental sculptural art survive from Whithorn, but Anglian styles of sculpture and ornamentation, characterised essentially by the animated vine-scroll, dominate from Nithsdale and Hoddom to Abercorn on the Forth. Anglian sculpture is pre-eminently represented, of course, in the famous crosses of Ruthwell in Dumfriesshire and Bewcastle in Cumberland, with their naturalistic mediterranean figures and their Northumbrian decorative motifs. It always seems odd that these masterpieces should be on the borders of Northumbria, but perhaps major works elsewhere in more developed areas have been destroyed. It is not easy to delineate any evolving British strand among the surviving monuments of North Britain. It may be that much British monumental art has been destroyed, or perhaps the Britons mainly drew on the artistic ideas of neighbouring peoples. Apart perhaps from the odd fragments with interlace decoration not particularly Anglian in character, the sculptured stones of Govan, for example, an important British artistic centre on the lower Clyde – all date to after A.D. 900 and draw essentially on late Pictish or Anglian traditions with some Scandinavian (Viking) influence. The so-called 'disc-faced' or 'disc-headed' crosses of Galloway also belong to this age and are moulded by Irish and Viking styles, while south of the Solway, in the Lake District, at the same period, are some pure Viking pieces and the Scandinavian impact is dominant. Artistic links between these crosses of the Lake District and Galloway suggest contact by sea, cutting out the Solway basin and apparently placing that region for a time rather on the fringe of developments.

What made possible the cultural dominance of Northumbria was, not unexpectedly, the influence of the Northumbrian Church. The Synod of Whitby (664) by no means obliterated the formative Dalriadic influence on Northumbrian ecclesiastical life which retained a Celtic element that could accommodate itself to the administration of North Britain. Though the later medieval cathedral appears to have destroyed all traces of Ninian's foundation at Whithorn, Abercorn on the Forth, which was a Northumbrian bishopric from 681 to 685 for the temporarily subject Picts, was of Irish appearance and design and consisted basically of a large, roughly oval, enclosure. Whithorn was established as a see for the Britons of Galloway around 720 and survived as such into the ninth century. There were ecclesiastical contacts between the Northumbrians and the Picts and between the Northumbrians and the Scots, and the Northumbrians were instrumental in bringing the Picts and the Scots to an acceptance of the Roman Easter in the early eighth century. But on the Strathclyde Britons they could not prevail. It was not until 768 that the Britons in Wales accepted the Roman Easter. The date of Strathclyde's acceptance is unknown. In fact, very little as yet is known about the Church in Strathclyde. Only with the appointment and consecration of Bishop John in 1114–18 does a see at Glasgow clearly emerge.

The Northumbrian scholar, Bede, wrote in 731 that, though the Picts and the Scots were then at peace with the Angles, for the most part the Britons who were not under Northumbrian control opposed them through inbred hatred. These would be the Britons of the kingdom of Strathclyde. Feelings ran high on both sides. In 786 visiting papal legates to Northumbria reprimanded the Angles for adopting British fashions of dress, thereby imitating in this way the life of those whom they had always detested. For a time, in the 670s, the Britons of Strathclyde, together with the Picts and the Scots, had been under military subjection to the Northumbrians but this overlordship was ended when the Northumbrians were defeated by the Picts in 685 at *Nechtansmere* (Dunnichen). Bridei, king of the Picts, the man responsible for the victory at *Nechtansmere,* was a son of Bile, formerly king of Strathclyde. The Strathclyde Britons for long played a significant part in the power politics of the North. It was the Strathclyde Britons under King Teudebur who defeated the seemingly invincible Pictish King Oengus in 750; and it was necessary for Oengus to ally with the Northumbrians to avenge this insult. The Northumbrians annexed the plain of Kyle in Ayrshire, however, and it is likely that Dalriadic Scots were migrating into British territory before Kenneth mac Alpin conquered the Picts. A daughter of Kenneth mac Alpin married Run, the son of Artgal, king of Strathclyde, and Run's son, Eochaid, was joint king of the Scots from 878 to 889 with Giric son of Dungal. This reversal to the Pictish principle of succession through the mother is strange. Perhaps Constantine I, son of Kenneth, had such a danger to the male line in mind when he was responsible for the slaying of King Artgal in 872. By no means all the names of the kings of Strathclyde in this period are known. The only dynastic pedigree to survive from Strathclyde is that which traces the ancestry of Run, son of Artgal, back through Teudebur and Bile to Ceretic.

One early Irish writer described the capture of York in Northumbria by the Vikings in 866 as the beginning of great suffering and misfortune for the Britons. In 870 Dumbarton was indeed captured by the Vikings after a siege of four months and its riches and countless captives taken away. On the whole, however, Strathclyde itself seems to have been on the sideline of Viking movements. It must have been the Britons particularly of what is now south-west Scotland who suffered most. As late as 875 the bishop of Lindisfarne and his community were in the vicinity of Whithorn, attempting unsuccessfully to obtain a crossing into Ireland and greater safety. They returned to Bernicia, and established their bishopric first at Chester-le-Street and then in 990 at Durham. But after 875 a darkness falls on Galloway which is primarily illuminated by the evidence of place-names. These reveal that from around 900 onwards Norse settlers were striking into this region from south of the Solway, together with Irish-speaking immigrants from Ireland known as the Gall-ghaedhil (foreign Gael) who gave their name to Galloway. There must have been quite a ferment. If the archaeologist could wish for some of the Dumbarton riches of 870, so the historian could wish for a detailed contemporary account of what was happening in Galloway and Dumfriesshire in the early tenth century. On the one hand, Viking art is conspicuous. On the other, a dynasty, which seems to have been predominantly Irish, must have established itself, for in 1034 is recorded the death of Suibne, son of Kenneth, king of the Galwegians. In addition, the tenth and eleventh centuries, again judging from the evidence of place-names, witnessed a British resurgence both in Galloway and Dumfriesshire and in the Lake District, south of the Solway, suggesting that Britons were also moving into these areas from Strathclyde and colonising afresh among the Vikings and the Irish. And, finally, there were the Scots.

Galloway was not to come securely under the control of the Scottish kings until the 1160s, but the threat to Strathclyde and the Lake District from the successors of Kenneth mac Alpin was more immediate. The MacAlpin kings had conquered what had been Southern Pictland in the mid-ninth century but it is doubtful if they exercised any real authority north of the Mounth, over Moray. They therefore looked southwards for expansion. By the reign of Indulf (954–62), Edinburgh had been re-occupied. Further territory in Lothian was ceded to Kenneth II around 973 and in 1018 the Scots, probably under the personal leadership of Malcolm II, won a great victory over the Bernicians at Carham on the

Tweed which established the Tweed as the new frontier. Northumbrian Angles north of the Tweed would either flee south or become absorbed within the Scottish kingdom. Malcolm's successors repeatedly tried to advance further. Duncan I, his grandson, carried out an abortive attack on Durham, not long before he was slain in Moray in 1040 by Macbeth. Duncan's son, Malcolm III (1057–93), who was able to make capital out of the Saxon resistance to the Normans in the north after the battle of Hastings, ravaged as far south as the Tees and the Cleveland hills. But no permanent success was ever achieved beyond the Tweed, not even by David I or William the Lion. A similar process of territorial expansion went on in the west and it was this which affected Strathclyde.

The native ruling family of Strathclyde may not even have survived the death, between 900 and 943, of Donald, king of the Britons, for his successor is named as Donald, son of Aed, in all probability the brother of the reigning king of the Scots, Constantine II, son of Aed. If the medieval chronicler, John of Fordun, is to be trusted at this point, Donald was succeeded by his son, Owen, and in this way Strathclyde passed under the control of an off-shoot of the Scottish dynasty. In 945, in an attempt to obtain a peace settlement with the Scots, Edmund, king of Wessex, granted Cumbria to Malcolm I, king of the Scots, on condition that Malcolm become his helper by land and sea. But what was ceded? Cumbria, from *Cumbri* (fellow countrymen), was a name which could be applied to Strathclyde. Indeed, the British language of this whole region is known to linguists as 'Cumbric'. Strathclyde and Cumbria, in fact, were used interchangeably. Now in 945 Edmund had recently sustained a serious onslaught from the Vikings at York and had only just managed to push his way northwards; he can have been in no position to cede the valley of the Clyde to the king of the Scots, whose kinsmen were probably in a strong position there already. Edmund must have granted land south of the Solway, in modern Cumberland. The boundaries of this Lakeland province appear to have been the Rerecross on Stainmoor and the river Duddon to the south. This would be a strategic area for intercepting Viking communications between Ireland and Man, Galloway and Yorkshire. It was later Scottish tradition that heirs-apparent to the Scottish kingdom were given British territory to govern. The descendants of Owen for their part did not press their claims to the MacAlpin kingship but hostility was latent. In 971 Culen, king of the Scots, was slain, probably at Abington, by Rhydderch, brother of Donald, son of Owen, king of Strathclyde. The two families were demonstrably drifting apart. When the heirs-apparent of the MacAlpin kings were sent to reign among the Britons, therefore, they must have gone elsewhere than to Strathclyde proper, and the likelihood is that they went to the British lands south of the Solway. The last king of Strathclyde was probably Owen the Bald, son of Donald. When he died in 1015, this particular branch of the MacAlpin family, which had been making Strathclyde their own, evidently died out or failed to maintain itself. It was in consequence probably the whole British area of Strathclyde, as well as the lands south of the Solway, which Malcolm II granted to his intended heir, Duncan; and it is significant corroboration of this general extension of Scottish influence into British territories that Malcolm III, son of Duncan, is styled in a twelfth century Anglo-Norman chronicle, frequently using older material, as 'son of the king of the Cumbrians'. Moreover, Gaelic place-names in Strathclyde, some representing settled, others pastoral, communities, appear to go back long before 1015 and spread steadily outwards across Lothian. Early Scottish settlement of this area was of quite significant proportions.

The arrangement with King Edmund afforded the Scots a very desirable footing south of the Solway, and helps to explain their eagerness to acquire land along the east coast, possibly to the Tees. To have successfully annexed all this territory would have created a very different Scotland from that which did emerge. Had this southern land been permanently acquired, there might have been no determined drive by later Scottish kings to assert their authority over Moray and the Gaelic uplands. It was the repulse from England which threw the Scottish kings back at the highland massif. The new Norman knights were like storm-troopers, for whom neither the Saxons, nor the Welsh, nor the Scots were a match. In 1092 William II (Rufus), king of England, came north to Carlisle and fixed the Solway as his northern boundary. Again, like the Tweed, this line of demarcation was never to be effectively challenged. The next year Malcolm III perished in a skirmish at Alnwick. The Scottish kingdom plunged into civil war to emerge under the sons of Malcolm and Margaret insecure at home and under embarrassing vassalage abroad to the Norman kings of England. The sons of Margaret were still lords of Cumbria above the Solway before succeeding as kings of the Scots, and it was the introduction of feudal tenure and the creation of a territorial diocese at Glasgow by David as earl of Cumbria in the period 1107–24 which opened up this British region, before any other part of Scotland, to the impact of Norman French society.

Archaeological advances are greatly extending our knowledge of the early British church in North Britain or in what is now southern Scotland. The science of place-name study is revealing, ever more clearly, the movements of peoples and the origin of incoming settlers. The historical records take us some way towards reconstructing the essentially dynastic history of Strathclyde. But we need to know much more about the later history of the Church in these British areas from the eighth to the eleventh century, and much more about the secular and material culture of the Britons before we can fully appreciate the significance of native Scottish influence on the general development of the region that was to become the launch-pad for the introduction of feudalism into Medieval Scotland. Here, in field work and topographical survey, as throughout all Scotland, the enthusiasm of local societies, in co-operation with the technical skills of archaeologists, historical geographers and historians, can make a very real and vital contribution.

CHAPTER VII

The Early Christian Church

Charles Thomas

Christianity, seen as one of several Mediterranean religions introduced to Britain in Roman times rather than as the revelation of Divine truth, began to affect Scotland at a comparatively late phase; and its initial progress there was slow. This does not impute any special strength to heathendom, in this case the polytheistic beliefs surviving from later prehistory. It is more likely to reflect the difficult internal communications, and sparsely-populated state, of the country, two conditions inimical to the rapid diffusion of any new idea.

The profound changes in Scottish life between (say) Calgacus and the Caledonians in the first century A.D., and Queen Margaret and her circle in the eleventh, could be attributed to a variety of factors – some demographic, others political or even climatic. The contribution of Christianity to this process, here as elsewhere, is most readily detected in the sphere of literacy, language, craftsmanship, and the social order. Despite the relative paucity of documentation, we can none the less reconstruct in rough outline the story of Scotland in Early Christian times, since much of it can be inferred from the evidence of archaeology and the history of art. In this chapter, a personal version of such a reconstruction will be offered, but in the guise of historical narrative, not as a disjointed catalogue of archaeological details.

The first individual Christians in Scotland may very probably have been legionaries, auxiliaries, or camp-followers, from the eastern provinces of the Roman Empire, as early as the second century. As individuals, they have left no trace. Our story properly commences a little later, around the close of the fourth century, and in the person of Scotland's first saint, Ninian. The earliest record of Ninian of Whithorn (whose real name was perhaps *Niniavus*) occurs in Bede's great Ecclesiastical History early in the eighth century; and the passage has to be appreciated in its true context. A little before 700, the Angles of Northumbria – that vigorous and gifted people to whom Bede himself belonged – had pushed their kingdom westwards across what are now Dumfries and Galloway. They had therefore acquired in the process several existing religious centres, including Whithorn in Wigtownshire. Bede is retailing a tradition then current at Whithorn (where the community might well have included British, Anglian, and even Irish brethren) which he would have received from some such correspondent as Pecthelm, the Anglian bishop. Bede tells us that 'Nynia' was a Briton, a bishop who had been regularly instructed in the faith 'at Rome' (in the Roman manner?), and that he had built at Whithorn a church of stone called, in Latin, *Ad Candidam Casam*, 'At the White House'. This church and the bishop's see were named in honour of St Martin. While modern students discount any direct connection with Martin of Tours, who died in the 390s, the general ambience of Ninian's career as portrayed in two later sources – a narrative miracle poem of the late eighth century and Ailred of Rievaulx's life in the twelfth – would support a late fourth century date.

Was this the first Christian settlement in Scotland? Why should it have been at Whithorn? Archaeology provides partial answers. The long coastal shelf of Dumfries and Galloway, as the distributions of Roman coins and small finds now show, was increasingly inhabited during the Roman centuries by people conversant with Roman material culture. Expansion westwards into this fertile tract from the great border settlement at Carlisle, and refugees from the major barbarian assaults on Hadrian's Wall and its hinterland, might be among the explanations for a pattern which looks like more than merely the outcome of trade. Recent excavations below the east end of Whithorn Priory church revealed, under the medieval burials and infill and under still earlier burials of the Anglian period, the crushed remnants of an east-west long cist cemetery of Early Christian character, itself apparently having disturbed cremations associated with Romano-British pottery. A native, part-Romanised settlement at Whithorn in the third century, embracing Christianity during the fourth, petitioning for its own bishop (from Carlisle?) late in that century, and being supplied (from the same source?) with Ninian who constructed his original church in the now-Christian local burial ground, is a hypothesis which would accord with these slender archaeological and historical clues.

During the next two centuries, almost all our evidence for any Christian life (or death) is drawn from south of the Forth-Clyde line, in the form of inscribed memorial tombstones. These can be very approximately dated by the style of the Roman capital lettering, by the evolution of a basic Christian motif called the *chi-rho* (anagram of the first two Greek capital letters of *Christos*, 'The Anointed One', like our modern plus-sign with a looped or hooked top arm), and by precise linguistic forms of some British Celtic personal names. The distributions shows us a rather leisurely spread from south to north – from the later fifth century in the Rinns and Whithorn, to the beginning of the seventh just south of the Forth – and at least one such stone, that at Yarrowkirk which names two local princes, implies a measure of success in converting the ruling families of the region.

What kind of church organisation does this indicate? Ninian was a bishop. A stone from Kirkmadrine in the Rinns of Galloway names two *sacerdotes* – literally 'priests' but at this period equally translatable as 'bishops' – and two more from the Peebles area, one long since lost and known to us only from a medieval report, actually mention *episcopi*, 'bishops'. We sense the force of Bede's remark that, as he puts it, Ninian had been 'regularly instructed'. This is a diocesan and episcopal church, like the Church of Rome, and later, the Episcopal Church in Scotland. One might take a further, tentative, step and suggest from the groupings of these early memorials, as well as from early traditions and place-names attached to selected churches, that diocesan areas did exist at this stage. If so, there is some general correspondence to what we believe to have been the secular tribal areas, by now the post-Roman kingdoms of North Britain – Strathclyde, Gododdin, Rheged, and in the long basin of the Tweed a lost kingdom which may underlie the *Bernicia* of Anglian Northumbria.

North of the Forth-Clyde line, some at least of the Picts may have been introduced to Christianity; even if we now find it hard to credit unreservedly Bede's statement that the southern Picts (the Picts living south of Aberdeen and the Mounth) had been converted by Ninian in person, harder still to accept more recent views which would make Ninian a peripatetic missionary roaming as far afield as the Moray Firth and the Northern Isles. On this eastern coast, the ascertained distribution of large lay cemeteries containing oriented long cist graves, a few of which are demonstrably sixth century and the majority of which are certainly Christian, spreads north of the Lothians around the coast of Fife and the mouth of the Tay. Are these the graveyards of scattered communities of Christian Picts? Was Abernethy, certainly a church site of great antiquity, founded in this context? On the west coast, if we choose to accept that the king Coroticus to whom, about 450, St Patrick of Ireland addressed a minatory epistle was the ruler of Strathclyde with his citadel at Dumbarton Rock, then we must face an implication. Patrick compares the soldiers of Coroticus (who had recently slain or enslaved some Christian converts) with 'the Scots and apostate Picts', i.e. with barbarians. If 'apostate' here means anything stronger than just 'un-Christian', it implies backsliding from a notionally converted state; and this, if located at all, would surely be on the north bank of the Clyde.

In the Glasgow region during the latter part of the sixth century we encounter our second realistic figure, Kentigern or Mungo, today mainly remembered as the patron of Glasgow's magnificent cathedral. There is no cause to reject the entry in a somewhat later North British chronicle, the *Annales Cambriae*, that notes the death of *Conthigirn(us)* under the year 612. In the medieval Life of the saint by Jocelin of Furness, the original graveyard surrounding the first church on the site of St Mungo's is claimed to have been consecrated by St Ninian. If by this we understand 'founded in connection with the diocesan episcopal church stemming from Ninian and Whithorn' I see no real reason to reject this tradition either.

In fifth century Ireland, the Patrician church, as with the sister church in western Britain (Cumbria, Wales, and the south-west), seems to exhibit a diocesan episcopal character. Its links were transmarine, with the church in Gaul, to a lesser extent with Spain, and in some important respects directly with the Mediterranean. At the end of the fifth century, a very different kind of Christian outlook, born in the desert lands around the East Mediterranean, was transmitted to the British Isles. Monks (*monachi*, 'solitaries'), in the sense of individual Christians who had taken personal vows of poverty or chastity or solitude, formed an early feature of Christian life. Communities of such monks sharing a communal existence with components of work, worship, prayer, education, and missionary activity grew partly out of enforced retreat to the deserts in the face of Roman persecution (before A.D. 313), and partly – notably as the movement's popularity gained ground – out of complex reactions to the worldliness of the Church under the later Empire. In such monasteries, the abbot and not the bishop was ruler, and provision for lay Christians was not on planned territorial lines. A diocesan structure involving bishops who controlled defined diocesan areas from fixed urban sees became increasingly irrelevant to those adhering to monastic ideals.

It is now highly doubtful whether full monasticism, inspired by St Martin of Tours' two pioneer establishments in north-west Gaul, did first take root in British soil at Whithorn in the late fourth century. Whithorn does appear to have become a conventional monastery by Bede's day, but this change can be ascribed to Irish Christian activity in Galloway two centuries after Ninian. The small building whose restored foundations protrude from below the east end of Whithorn Priory is much more likely to have originated as a subsidiary monastic chapel in the seventh century than to represent Ninian's supposed 'church of stone'. Monasticism possesses its own distinctive field-archaeology, absent from earlier Whithorn, as it is also absent from Ireland during the fifth century. Where approximate dates can be supplied for the archaeological traces of our first monastic establishments, such dates are won with difficulty from fragments of wheel-made pottery from the Mediterranean imported alongside the fresh ideas of monasticism itself. On this score we detect, not surprisingly, a sea-borne spread from south to north. The earliest datable foundation (about 480 to 500) seems to be Tintagel on the north Cornish coast. Scarcely later are those on the south Welsh coast. A few decades later, we find monasteries in Ireland, particularly the Irish midland plain and its river-system extensions.

The picture is complicated by a non-religious factor, that of internal migrations and new colonies which took shape, in both Britain and Ireland, during the third to seventh centuries. Irish groups were settling in areas like Pembroke and Argyll, where new dynasties were founded. Friction between the incomers and existing populations must have been related to the availability of desirable land and to densities of settlement.

The settlement in western Scotland – historically of interest because the extra-national name of the Irish colonists (*Scotti*) later became applied to the whole region – must be seen in terms of migration in strength, late in the fifth century. It sprang from what is now Ulster. It was from this province also that Columba or Columcille, an aristocratic recruit to the first age of insular monasticism, was drawn. By the middle of the sixth century, the Dalriadic settlers (as they are known) in Argyll may have contained in their ranks descendants of Irish families first converted in Patrick's day; we do not know this, but it was in part to provide a religious focus for the settlement that Columba (born about 521) and his companions founded their monastery on Iona in A.D. 563.

While by no means the only extension of Irish monasticism to the Irish colonies – and we tend to overlook St Moluoc at Lismore, and later St Maelrubha at Applecross, to say nothing of less distinct figures working in west central and south-west Scotland – Iona was unquestionably the most influential. We possess a stylised Life of Columba written about 690, a century after Columba's death in 597, by Adomnan, the ninth abbot of Iona. A continuous connection was maintained with Ireland, whither indeed (at Kells, Co. Meath) the Iona community returned during the Norse on-slaughts of the early ninth century. There was a close relationship with the Dalriadic ruling houses, as well as external contact with royal circles in Pictland and Northumbria. Finally, the founder himself was, at various times, the subject of widespread cults involving church dedications, relics, and devotional literature.

We can fairly say, then, that Christianity in the far west and north of Scotland (including the Western and Northern Isles) stems in the main from 563 and later. Archaeologically it is repre-sented by a typical monastic church, with enclosed monasteries of varying size on islands, promontories and high ground; with isolated enclosed chapelries and cemeteries; with a huge series of grave-markers, cross-marked slabs, free-standing crosses and pillars; and with all the minor material culture of a missionary church.

While most natives would have been British speakers of ultimate prehistoric origin, ranging socially in far-flung communities from the descendants of prosperous broch-centred farmers to crofters and fishers at bare subsistence level, the Irish clerics and their parties would have encountered – probably in Skye, certainly in Orkney and Shetland – Pictish settlers spreading out from north-east Scotland. The Christian missionaries apparently contacted Orkney from the late sixth century, with Shetland somewhat later than this. At the height of the fashion for *deserta* and really isolated asceticism, many small islets hardly capable of supporting life were pressed into service as hermitages; still other Irish brethren sailed across near-Arctic seas as far as Faroe and Iceland, if not indeed further.

The conversion of the Picts, the political centre of whose loosely-strung kingdom was in Columba's time near Inverness, is historically ill-defined. Overlooking for the minute any earlier contacts between the church of St Ninian's day and the Picts in Fife, or Dunbartonshire, we do possess Adomnan's record of visits undertaken by Columba to the Pictish king, Bridei, and to districts 'across the ridge of Britain'. In the next hundred and fifty years, it is likely that Christianity spread slowly through Pictland on lines similar to those that we infer for the western seaboard, but we have no direct information; nor, in that extensive region south of the Moray Firth and north of the Tay, has the field-work necessary to establish the appropriate sites of such a missionary church yet been undertaken.

Northumbria, in the early seventh century, comprised two regions or sub-kingdoms – Bernicia in the north, and Deira in roughly part of Yorkshire. Dynastic quarrels had led to the exile of some Bernician princes, in Pictland or among the Irish settlers in Argyll. Oswald, who returned to unite the realm after a notable victory at Heavenfield (by Hadrian's Wall), must during the years 617 to 634 have had much contact with the Irish monastic mission. He spoke Old Irish, was presumably baptised, and may even have stayed at Iona. In 635, he resuscitated the spark of Christianity in Northumbria, of which more below, by inviting Aidan, an Irish monk from Iona, to act as bishop and to found a new monastery at Lindisfarne (Holy Island). The repercussions of this move went far beyond the following thirty years of Irish-type Christianity in this northern English kingdom.

In 597, St Augustine and his small mission, with the blessing of Pope Gregory the Great, had landed in Kent with the aim of converting the pagan English. Gregory's elaborate scheme for the division of the country into two provinces, Canterbury and York, with subordinate dioceses and an independent bishopric at London, was not in the event immediately realisable. Outside the relatively civilised kingdom of Kent, the only early extension took place as a result of a Christian Kentish princess marrying Edwin of Northumbria. The accompanying Christian entourage, headed by Paulinus, did succeed in baptising Edwin on Easter Day in 627, in supervising a mass baptism of the Deirans, and in building various churches; but Edwin's untimely death in battle a few years later and the pagan devastation which ensued virtually extinguished this little candle. When Christianity came again to Northumbria, it did so through Bernicia, not Deira, and not primarily as a diocesan episcopal church on orthodox Roman lines. There was a strong, perhaps dominant, element of monasticism derived from the western world of the ascetic and scholarly Irish church.

In lowland England, the 'regular' Roman church of the fourth century, as far as we can detect with its hierarchy and structure in line with Imperial practice, was almost entirely erased by the Anglo-Saxon settlements during the fifth century. Gregory and Augustine, through their mission, sought to re-establish this link with the metropolitan heartland. Success was eventually to crown their efforts, and we recall that the present constitution of the Church of England is broadly on this Gregorian model. In the powerful and brilliant Northumbria of the seventh century, however, it was not until the decisions of the Synod of Whitby in 663 (or 664) had been taken that the Northumbrian church turned finally towards Rome, the Continent, and in the direction of medieval Europe.

This is relevant to Scotland, particularly the Lowlands, about which it can be said that Edinburgh has been an English-speaking centre since the seventh century. Between 635 and 663, and probably later, whatever remained of the old Ninianic Christian province in the south of Scotland had been enriched by a variety of new monasteries within the ambit of Lindisfarne. In the case of at least two – Old Melrose in a bend of the Tweed, Abercorn just west of Edinburgh – it may be significant that these retained their British place-names throughout, instead of being given English ones (like Hexham, Jarrow, Whitby or Monkwearmouth). Were these two like Whithorn the diocesan churches of sub-Roman times?

The full circle of Irish influence, ecclesiastical contact and borrowings between Northumbria and Pictland, was not closed until a century later. There were certain procedural divergences between the Roman church, which stemmed continuously from the age of the apostles and the early Mediterranean centuries, and the so-called Celtic church, that early offshoot leaning towards monasticism and surviving in much of Ireland and parts of north and

G

west Britain. Apart from such minor questions as the shapes of clerical tonsures, the number of bishops needed regularly to consecrate a new bishop, and the method of computing annually the date of Easter, there was the wider problem of the status of bishops – in Celtic lay eyes not necessarily as important as abbots, and within the monasteries often subordinate to abbots who were not themselves also bishops. Bede, writing of Iona, could draw attention to the 'unusual arrangements' current there, in which 'the island has an abbot for ruler who is a priest, to whose authority all the kingdom, including even bishops, must be subject.'

It was, however, the controversy over Easter that influenced the course of the church in Pictland. In 663 or 664, at Whitby, the Northumbrian church moved to the Roman method of computing Easter, and presumably this would have held good within that part of Pictland – Fife, and some uncertain area northward – which from the mid-650s to 685 formed part of the Northumbrian kingdom as a result of conquest. The Pictish church must then, like Oswald's brother Oswiu and his royal wife Eanfled, have had the embarrassment of two distinct dates for Easter according to the way in which these had been reckoned.

In 685, after the notable Pictish victory at Nechtansmere in Angus, the Northumbrians were forced to retreat south of the Forth, abandoning Abercorn and other places. The Pictish church was left to its older parent, the Iona of Columba. About 690, however, Adomnan of Iona (who had twice visited Northumbria and enjoyed much prestige there) accepted the Roman method of computing Easter. Despite difficulties then raised at Iona, where the community did not follow suit until 716, Adomnan's action won over most of the Irish foundations. Around 710, the Picts, as Isabel Henderson has pointed out in a previous chapter, accepted the Roman Easter as well, and as if this were symbolic of entry into the wider world of the Roman church, cast off the ecclesiastical domination of Iona, expelling certain Columban monks. Whatever form the church in Pictland now assumed, and as a kingdom with some kind of tribal substructure it may well have moved in the direction of fixed territorial dioceses retaining monasteries only in distant and isolated areas, we can attach to this post-710 period a new phenomenon. This is the appearance of a very notable strain of artistic endeavour, especially in fine metalwork and relief sculpture, that brings into a single east-coast continuum not only

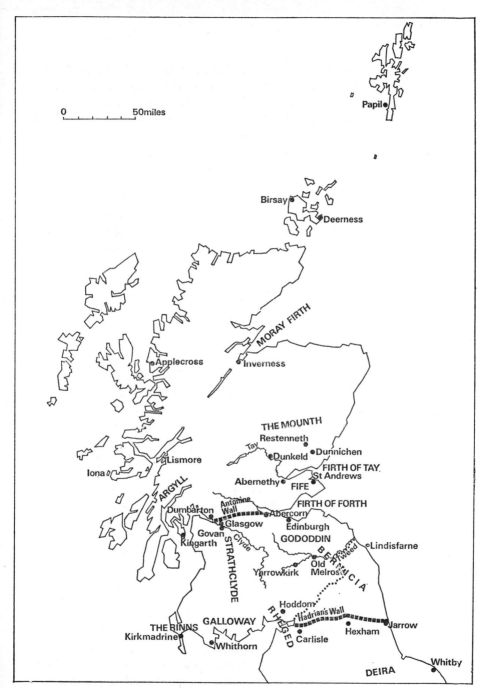

Fig 13   Early Christian centres

Northumbria, Pictland, the far north of Scotland and the Northern Isles, but also to the south the converted English kingdoms beyond the Humber and (through Northumbria) the Continent.

What has now become Scotland, then, on the eve of the first Norse raids and settlements around 800, presents to us a complex and fascinating picture of provincial Christianity – a picture drawn from a number of sources, and one which was built up through a series of fortuitous events. We have noted the fact that Oswald happened to be exiled within reach of Iona; the fact that one church chose to calculate Easter through a nineteen-year equinoctial cycle and another through an eighty-four year table; the fact that a late Romano-British community at Whithorn was in a position to have its own bishop; and (we could add) the fact that a type of monasticism evolved in the Eastern Mediterranean happened to fit into the social structure of Early Christian Ireland rather more readily than urban-centred dioceses. We can attempt a necessarily simplified summary of the position in the late eighth century.

From Galloway and Clyde-mouth, in a long ragged chain right up to the archipelagos of the far north, monasteries of varying importance from Iona downwards still flourished – ruled by abbots, and staffed by brethren of Scottish (i.e. Irish), North British, Pictish and even English descent. One might cite such cases as Whithorn itself, Kingarth in Bute, probably Govan, Iona, Lismore, Applecross, Birsay and Deerness in Orkney, and Papil in Shetland. Not all are known and fewer still are explored. A multitude of much smaller 'eremitic monasteries', with bare handfuls of monks, have to be added, together with isolated hermitages, the equivalent of mission stations in the shape of enclosed cemeteries with cells for clerics, and perhaps even the counterpart of later domestic chapels for ruling families. There is still no firm evidence that this remnant of western Christianity was, except in a very wide way, diocesan, and the old monastic *paruchia* (roughly, the enforceable sphere of influence of a given major monastery) may have been the practical unit.

Over most of Scotland, none the less, north of the Forth and Clyde, the church in Pictland is seen to be moving closer to regular episcopal foci (such as Abernethy, St Andrews, and perhaps Dunkeld) and to a corresponding diocesan structure. In southern Scotland, we see but the northern aspect of that portion of the English church connected with now-enlarged Northumbria; with some rearrangement of its dioceses, but since the Synod of Whitby closely in line with the Continent. To the west, that long-lived North British kingdom of Strathclyde, whose religious side found expression later still as the medieval diocese of Glasgow, alone has some claim to more or less continuous status, through the chair of Kentigern, from Ninianic times.

There are of course gaps in this picture. The Christian history and archaeology of disturbingly extensive areas (for example, Ayrshire, or the north-west beyond Argyll) is still hardly known. Nor was this a static picture. As with every other known church, maturity had brought its own problems, and earlier in the eighth century Bede had given hints of the need for reform in many ways. Asceticism would always possess some peculiar hold on the Celtic mind and the Culdee movement represented a peculiarly lasting off-shoot from Columban days and the first wave of monastic customs. In 795, Norse devastation commenced at Iona; internally, the Scots and the Picts were being nudged by historical currents to-wards a form of unity, attained first during the stormy reign of Kenneth mac Alpin in the middle of the ninth century. The church in Northumbria was itself an obvious target for Viking plunder, nowhere more so than in such exposed places as coastal Lindisfarne. Iona, despite Kenneth mac Alpin's adherence to the cult of Columba (he himself was buried there, and the Relig Oran graveyard seems first to have taken shape as a sacred en-closure on this occasion), entered a period of decline. Whithorn at the end of the ninth century became a momentary refuge for the monks of Lindisfarne who were attempting to flee to Ireland. It was on this occasion that the Lindisfarne Gospels, immersed in their shipwreck, were miraculously cast up on a beach near Whithorn; but after this, Whithorn too fades into obscurity, not relieved until the see was revived in the early twelfth century.

Above all, perhaps, we get the impression that in Scotland we have a clear case of the story of Christianity being in large measure inseparable from the country's political and social history. Despite our sadly inadequate knowledge of the parts played by individuals in this development, the impression is as true of Scotland between the Romans and the Vikings as it is of more recent centuries in Scottish history. The archaeology of this period, largely dominated by the remains of Christianity, is rich, exciting, informative and only imperfectly explored; further work cannot fail to throw much light on contemporary Ireland, Pictland and northern England. Of those names that we do know, Columba for sure, and one would like to think Ninian as well, must be placed besides Patrick and Augustine as Christian figures of destiny.

CHAPTER VIII

The Norsemen

David M. Wilson

There is to this day a community of taste and spirit between
Scotland and Norway which must owe its origin to the geographical
situation of Scotland in relation to the western seaboard of Scandinavia. Lerwick, in Shetland, is as close to Bergen as it is to
Aberdeen and, ever since the Viking Age, there has been constant
traffic between Norway and the mainland of Shetland – an island
which forms the first of a series of stepping-stones which trace the
path from the North to Scotland and to the Irish Sea. While there
are minimal traces of Scottish-Scandinavian contacts before the
Viking Age, such connections are not adequately documented
until the Norsemen arrived to raid and settle the rich lands to the
south.

The foreign activities of the Norsemen were many and varied;
their Scottish adventure was but one facet of their kaleidoscopic
career in most of the known world in the years between, say, 790
and 1080. In the east, Swedish traders reached towards Baghdad,
while in the west Danish kings felt strong enough to face the
military might of the empire of Charlemagne, and Norwegians
sailed the Atlantic, discovering America, Iceland and Greenland
and settling with greater or lesser success in most of the North
Atlantic islands. The Scottish career of the Norsemen was merely a
prolonged and varied episode in a complicated series of
manoeuvrings in which the Scandinavians sought to gain riches or
political power outside their own country. The story of the Norsemen in Scotland cannot be taken in isolation: reference must
continually be made to events both in Scandinavia and in other
western countries.

The evidence on which this story is based is often difficult to
evaluate. Although this is an historical period, and written sources
are available, some of these sources are more reliable than others.
Their quality naturally varies in a period of three hundred years.
In the ninth century, for instance, contemporary British sources
are often very one-sided: if we are to believe the *Annals of Ulster*,
for example, the most important late eighth – and early ninth –

century attacks on Scotland were those on the Christian monastery at Iona which was founded by St Columba. The annalists (probably because an Iona chronicle was used as a source by the Irish annalists) omit all references to attacks and settlements in the islands and in the northern areas of Scotland, attacks which we know from other sources to have taken place. It is unfortunate that, until the very end of the Viking Age, there are few Scottish historical sources for the Norse activities, while the Scandinavian sources (of which the most important is undoubtedly the *Saga of the Orkneys*) were mostly written down long after the events which they record, and must often be treated as less than reliable. Careful evaluation of the historical material – Anglo-Saxon, Irish, Scottish and Scandinavian – enables us, however, to build up an outline against which evidence from other fields of study can be laid. Two other disciplines – the study of place-names and archaeology – provide the only other major sources for the Norse settlements of Scotland. The former is, in Scotland, in an embryonic stage and the latter is extremely one-sided – only six major Norse settlement sites, for example, have been thoroughly excavated in Scotland (two in Shetland, three in Orkney and one in Caithness), whereas the sites of more than fifty graves or cemeteries have been recovered from the Norse areas of the country.

The reasons for Norse activity in Scotland were diverse and are obscured by lack of evidence. Basically, however, two traits can be discerned; firstly the acquisition of movable wealth which could be taken back to the homeland and, secondly, the acquisition of land for settlement. Neither must be over-emphasised and both could be carried on by one man in the course of his lifetime; in the *Saga of the Laxdalers*, for example, Ketil Flatnose said that, 'he preferred to go west across the sea to Scotland because, he said, he thought the living was good there. He knew the country well, for he had raided there extensively'.

The raiding activities of which Ketil spoke can occasionally be revealed by archaeology, both in Scotland and in Scandinavia. In Scandinavia, objects of Scottish manufacture found in ninth century graves reflect in some cases the raids of the first Vikings. It is sometimes difficult to distinguish between Irish and Scottish metalwork; but a number of Pictish brooches, for example, of the same form as those found in the St Ninian's Isle treasure, have been uncovered in ninth-century Norwegian graves and tell of Viking adventures overseas. In Scotland the graves of the Norse raiders and traders tell of the early years of their appearance in this country, while the hoards of treasure reflect the story of their three hundred year period of high influence. The St Ninian's Isle hoard, buried in the last years of the eighth century or in the early years of the ninth century, was presumably one of the earliest treasures hidden against the initial Norse onslaught. Like such hoards as those from Croy in Inverness-shire and Rogart in Sutherland, it was probably hidden by a Pictish family at the time of a threatened attack and never reclaimed because of the death or captivity of the original owners.

The later hoards (hoards like that from Skaill in Orkney, which contained a large number of silver penannular brooches, as well as coins which date its deposition to about 950) may well represent the family treasure of a settler in the new lands who fell victim to some internecine Norse quarrel of a type often recounted in the Scandinavian sources. Nearly thirty hoards of the Viking Age have been found in Scotland, but the vast majority belong to the latter category, and probably only about three to the St Ninian's Isle group. The hoards, however, indicate the troubled nature of the times and by their distribution show the areas that most interested the Scandinavians – namely the northern and western islands, the west coast and the most northerly counties of the Scottish mainland.

A similar and perhaps more significant pattern is demonstrated by the distribution of Norse graves in Scotland. These are all found within the same area and no graves are found on the east coast south of the Moray Firth, with the exception of a single burial at Errol in Perthshire. Examination of Norse place-names has shown a like distribution and indicates clearly that the Scandinavian settlers never permanently penetrated the rich heart of Pictland – the area that became the kernel of the Scottish kingdom after the Dalriadic Scottish king, Kenneth mac Alpin, with the aid of Norse relatives and friends from the west and from Dublin, conquered the remains of the Pictish kingdom in a long series of campaigns in the mid-ninth century.

The graves have an added interest in that their contents show the type of people who came from Scandinavia to die in Scotland. The objects found in the burials show that they represent the first hundred years of the Norse presence and, although the vast

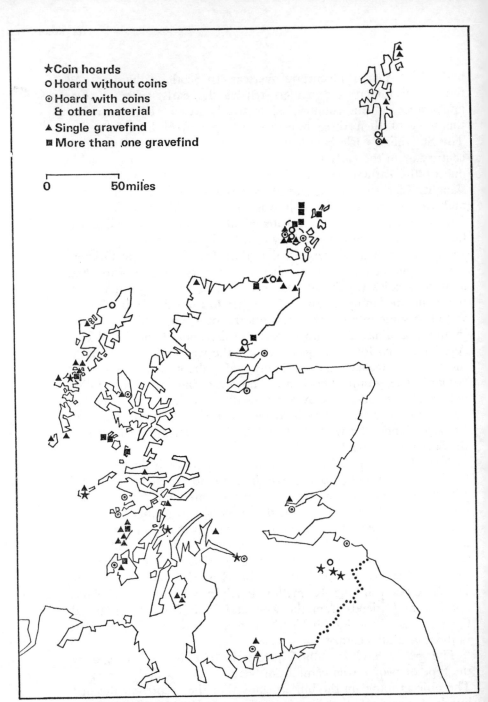

Legend:

★ Coin hoards
○ Hoard without coins
⊙ Hoard with coins & other material
▲ Single gravefind
▣ More than one gravefind

0   50 miles

Fig 14   Viking hoards and graves in Scotland

majority are male graves containing weapons, a good number are the graves of women who wore Scandinavian fashions. The Norsemen, then, were already confident enough in the early ninth century to begin to bring their women to Scotland and to settle the new lands, permanently. Most of the graves are found singly : cemeteries are rare and only at Pierowall on the Orkney Island of Westray has a substantial cemetery been recognised (17 graves have been established from existing records, perhaps twice that number have been uncovered at the site since the eighteenth century). No Scottish grave can be dated to the tenth century and we may assume that, as elsewhere in the Norse areas of Britain, the settlers gradually adopted Christianity and eschewed their ancient pagan customs of which the most obtrusive archaeologically was the rite of burial with grave goods. There is a hint at one or two sites, particularly at Ackergill (where one of the graves in a cemetery contained a chain of Norse type), that the Norse adopted the cist-grave inhumation rite of the native population and also respected Christian burial places – a feature which is paralleled, for example, in the Isle of Man. At a much later date – in the eleventh century – a few grave-stones decorated with Scandinavian ornament were set up (examples have been found at Kibar on Barra and at Dòid Mhàiri, Port Ellen, Islay); such monuments are, however, very uncommon. From such material it is clear that already in the ninth century the Norsemen were settled in the areas which they held until the collapse of Norwegian power in Scotland.

There are many indications that they were willing to adopt features from their new country. Although they brought their own law, they were willing to adopt a new religion, Christianity, and even early in the Norse period we have seen how they adopted and respected Christian burial practices. In minor things they were also influenced by local conditions; although they brought their own women with them they soon adopted local fashion in dress; the British ring-headed pin, for instance, is a common dress-fastener in Scottish Norse graves.

Norse settlement sites are also found but it is hard to generalise concerning them as most of the finds are from the northern Isles or the northernmost counties. Excavations at present being conducted by Dr Iain Crawford in North Uist may well produce evidence of Scandinavian settlement in the Western Isles, but, although a number of sites in this area have been identified in the past as Norse, this site is the first one to provide more than a hint of Scandinavian influence. On the other hand, a site in Shetland, romantically named Jarlshof by Sir Walter Scott, provides us with one of the most completely excavated Scandinavian settlements in the west Norse world.

Like its Norwegian and Icelandic counterparts, Jarlshof is a large farm (villages were apparently rare in Norse areas at this period) and is set on the edge of a bay with a gently shelving beach (ideally suited for drawing up ships) on the southern tip of the mainland of Shetland. The site has a long history, for it was continuously occupied from the seventh century B.C. until the last house to be built there was sacked by the notorious Earl Patrick Stewart in 1609. Excavations of a desultory sort were carried out at the site during the early years of this century, but systematic excavation was not started until the 1930s and by the time the site was completely cleared, shortly after the Second World War, a considerable complex of buildings of Viking Age date had been uncovered.

Basically the Viking Age site was a single farm. In its earliest phase (dated to the first half of the ninth century by the excavator) the farm consisted of a long dwelling house, 70 ft. x 20 ft., with slightly bowed sides divided into two rooms and with a central hearth in the main room, the hall. At some distance from the house were a series of byres and other ancillary buildings, all enclosed by a boundary wall which survived from the pre-Viking Age settlement of the site. The house is adequately paralleled in other Atlantic communities – in Iceland, for example, or in Greenland – and was presumably the house of a reasonably wealthy family. That the family became more prosperous is indicated by the gradual development of the farm over the next four hundred years; the buildings being added to or repaired and the whole dwelling house being ultimately replaced by a completely new structure, until, in the final phase, an elaborate house and a number of out-buildings were clustered together and surrounded by the tumble-down ruins of earlier structures.

The farm was self-supporting and the excavator has suggested that, from a pastoral-agricultural economy in the early phases of the settlement, fishing began to play a more dominant role in the eleventh century, for line and net sinkers are found in some numbers in the later period of the Norse farm. A certain number of exotic objects of Scandinavian or Scottish origin were found in the course of the excavations, but the vast majority of the large number of finds reflect the humdrum round of everyday life – cooking pots of soapstone, querns, sickle blades, pins, spindle whorls for spinning, and so on. The great quantity of soapstone on the site reflects a major industry of the Viking Age, for, at a period when the rest of Europe was using pottery, people of the western Scandinavian areas made elaborate vessels from soapstone. Traces of a soapstone quarry, in which the cores of soapstone bowls are still to be seen in the living rock, have been recognised some fifteen miles north of Jarlshof at Cunningsburgh, and it is possible that some of the objects quarried here found their way to Jarlshof and even further afield.

Objects made of soapstone are also found in great quantities at the only other Norse settlement so far excavated in Shetland, at Underhoull on Unst, the most northerly island of the archipelago. This farm seems to have been built in the early ninth century on the site of a pre-existing settlement, and may well have survived

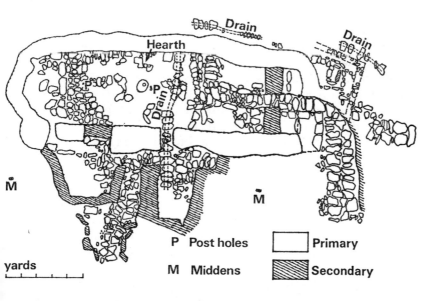

Fig 15 *Norse longhouse at Underhoull, Unst, Shetland*

for two or more centuries. The main building consisted of at least two rooms in a long house rather smaller than that at Jarlshof (measuring 55 ft. x 15 ft.). Although the site was by no means as rich in finds as Jarlshof, its size and situation, near to the shore in a small bay in Lunda Wick, together with the fact that it is situated on the edge of one of the most fertile areas in Unst, would suggest that the family who farmed here were reasonably substantial farmers even though they may not have had the wealth or social position of their Jarlshof contemporaries.

Farms of comparable status have also been excavated at three other sites in Scotland, at Skaill in Deerness and at Aikerness in Orkney, as well as at Freswick in Caithness. But the most important settlement site other than Jarlshof is the great complex of structures on Birsay, a tidal islet off the north-west tip of the Mainland of Orkney. Here, on the site of an early Christian monastery was established a farm which ultimately grew into a complex establishment consisting at one time of the palace of Earl Thorfinn (who died there in 1065) and later of the palace and cathedral of the Bishop of Orkney. The site was finally downgraded when the new cathedral in Kirkwall received the shrine of its Patron Saint, St Magnus, from Birsay in the middle of the twelfth century. By then the Earl was already living in his castle in Kirkwall and, although the Bishop retained a major house on the mainland opposite the islet of Birsay, he too was soon to move nearer to his cathedral. With a few insignificant exceptions no building took place on the site after 1200 and the work of archaeologists has revealed an unique series of buildings, both secular and lay, which span the whole of the Norse period.

Unfortunately, the finds from the site have not been published and a discussion of the excavation is only available in a most summary form so that any description can only convey a rough idea of the building sequence. On the slope above the foundations of the stone-built cathedral, outside the area recognised as the bishop's palace and a little to the south of it, are preserved today two houses exactly equivalent to those found at Jarlshof and elsewhere; the excavator has implied that they formed part of a complex of a ninth-century farm. If this is the case, it is interesting that the settlers respected the site of the pre-existing church (we know it is a church from various inscribed and decorated Pictish stones); perhaps they buried their dead in the cemetery alongside the bodies of the previous owners; whether such be the case or not the church preserved its identity and it ultimately became the site of the cathedral of the diocese. Here can be seen that respect for sacred places, even if they were not of the pagan Norse religion, which has been noticed earlier and which is an outstanding feature both in Scotland and in other lands settled by Scandinavian invaders. The new church was endowed in the middle of the eleventh century by Earl Thorfinn the Mighty on his return from a pilgrimage to Rome. A range of buildings form, together with the church, a square courtyard partially surrounded by a cemetery. These buildings – which may be interpreted as the bishop's palace – seem to have been built in the twelfth century. A major building complex to the east, partly collapsed into the sea, may represent the remains of the Earl's house, for we know that Earl Thorfinn, for example, spent a good deal of time here. The interpretation of the various buildings on the site – some of which are large and very impressive – is a matter of controversy, but two large halls have been tentatively identified.

Birsay is a splendid memorial to the wealth of the Orkney earldom in the period of Norse rule; but other uninvestigated sites, such as that at Westness on Rousay, may yet reveal impressive buildings – at least as large as those found at Birsay. Birsay is the only place in the Norse world where a semi-royal and episcopal complex survives. Gardar in Greenland provides us with the only comparable episcopal site so far excavated.

No site remotely resembling Birsay has been found on the west coast of Scotland or in the Western Isles – indeed such sites probably never existed. Iona functioned from time to time as a bishop's seat during the Norse period, but the cathedral of the diocese was at Peel in the Isle of Man (the title of the Manx bishopric – Sodor and Man – to this day enshrines the Norse bishopric, the word 'Sodor' referring to the *Suthreyjar*, the southern isles or Hebrides). Little of Norse origin remains at Iona other than a runic inscription, the odd grave slab carved in a Scandinavian style and the graves of a few kings of the Isles. The politics of western Scotland in the Norse period are complicated, as the area seems to have been under the nominal control of different people at different times, the King of Dublin, the King of Man and the Earl of Orkney being the chief contenders for the overlordship of the area. We may presume that there were grand houses –

even royal houses, like that of Somerled of Argyll – in the area, but they have never been identified archaeologically and even more humble Norse dwellings have not been recognised. We have seen how the graves and hoards demonstrate a firm Scandinavian presence in the west and there seems little reason to doubt the strategic importance of this area in relation to the important mercantile route between Norway and Dublin. The settlers of the islands and of the west coast and their descendants controlled this major trade artery and drew their wealth from it.

The Viking Age proper is considered as finished by the end of the eleventh century, but Norwegian political power continued in various parts of Scotland until much later. The Hebrides – with Man – were abandoned to the Scottish crown as late as 1266. The Northern Isles were officially Norwegian for an even longer period. Orkney was pledged to the Scottish crown for 50,000 Rhenish florins in 1468 as part of the cash dowry of Margaret, daughter of Christian I and wife of James III; while in 1469, in connection with the same marriage, Shetland was pledged for 8,000 florins. Neither pledge was redeemed. But long before any of these events people who lived in areas which had once been under Scandinavian control considered themselves as Hebridean, as Shetlanders or as men of Argyll, not as Norsemen; they hardly considered themselves as Scots – many of them to this day are, for example, Orcadians first and Scots second. In Shetland the view is expressed that all that ever came from Scotland was 'dear meal and greedy ministers'.

It is in Orkney and Shetland that the Scandinavian element in Scotland's make-up is still seen to this day. Not because there are a large number of huge blonde 'Vikings' in these islands – this well-fostered image seems ludicrous even to the casual observer – but there are many minor contacts. An Orkney drifter's skipper will listen to the Norwegian weather forecast – in Norwegian. Scots-women are often met with in west-coast fisher communities in Norway, married out of Kirkwall or Scalloway. A Norwegian lifeboat is stationed in Lerwick and there are Norwegian consulates in the islands. If one digs deeper one finds more fundamental traces of Scandinavian contact : the ancient Norse 'udal' law of the Northern Isles is still occasionally upheld in the Scottish Courts, and the names of tools and fishing equipment have a Scandinavian ring. Until 250 years ago a language – Norn – was spoken in the Northern Isles which was basically a Scandinavian tongue.

For Scotland as a whole, however, the traces of Scandinavian influence can easily be explained by the geographical setting of the two areas on the edge of the Atlantic. Place-names, loan words and church dedications are the only real survivals of the Viking Age. Other features are no more significant of an 800-year-old contact than is the presence of an Icelandic consul in present-day Edinburgh. Those who would argue to the contrary can only be accused of romanticism.

CHAPTER IX

Anglo-French Influences
G. W. S. Barrow

Macbeth, the warrior king who nevertheless found time to journey to Rome and 'scatter his money like seed to the poor', brought the first Norman knights to Scotland. Refugees from the Anglo-Welsh border country, they fought for Macbeth at the Battle of Dunsinnan Hill (1054) and were cut down by the king's rival and supplanter, Malcolm Canmore, and his Northumbrian allies. The Scots cannot have been much impressed by these newcomers, with their hauberks and war-trained horses, any more than were the Irish by the sight of their first Norman invaders a century later : 'ninety heroes dressed in mail, and the Gaels put little store by them'. The Scots learned their mistake sooner, though not quicker, than the Irish. Already in 1072 King Malcolm had met the greatest of all the Normans, William the Conqueror, at the ancient Pictish centre of Abernethy on the Tay, only a few miles south of the spot where Osbern 'surnamed Pentecost' and Hugh and their unnamed fellow-Normans had been slain. There, in the presence of the great host William had brought from the south, the king of Scots bowed to the duke of the Normans – now five years king of conquered England – and became his vassal. There was no Scottish Hastings, and the Normans attempted neither to dislodge the native dynasty nor to take over the country. But from 1072 until the death of the last of the Conqueror's sons in 1135 the kings of Scotland danced for the most part to the Normans' tune.

The ascendancy of the Normans from 1050 to 1150 was a European phenomenon which has never been satisfactorily explained. In the course of this century the Normans had made themselves practically the equal of the kings of France in their own small duchy and actually masters of Sicily, southern Italy, England, Scotland and much of Wales, and they had played a decisive part in the great Frankish push into the Near East and the lands of the old Roman Empire based on Byzantium. Within another thirty years they had added Ireland to their list of conquests. Scotland might have been conquered and overrun by them, as befell England; penetrated piecemeal with a long series of conquests in miniature, as happened in Wales; or half-conquered, without full assimilation, as proved to be the fate of Ireland. In any event, Scotland could never ignore the Normans, nor be ignored by them. But what in fact occurred was not complete conquest, nor piecemeal conquest, nor half-conquest. Through the dynasty of Malcolm Canmore (which was able to hold the Scottish throne almost without a break from 1058 to 1290), Scotland came to terms with the Normans. It is true that they were in the ascendant politically and militarily for ninety years (1124–1214); but it was an ascendancy under the Crown, a Crown which never completely ceased, even in its most 'normanised' phase (1153–1200), to be responsive to native custom and native political institutions. Consequently, Scotland was never brought permanently within the ambit of a continental empire (the fifteen years' explicit overlordship of Henry of Anjou, 1174–1189, was not typical), nor did French ever become the universal official language, as it did, for example, in England. All through the twelfth and thirteenth centuries the real linguistic struggle in the Scottish kingdom was not against French but between the two principal native vernaculars, a form of northern English ('Scots'), which eventually won, and a form of Irish ('Scottish Gaelic'), which eventually lost. It is noticeable that when in the late thirteenth and early fourteenth centuries the Scots government wished to correspond with the French government they wrote in Latin; only when communicating with the English government did they have recourse to French, or what passed for French south of the border.

When we use the name 'Normandy' we call to mind the pleasantly rolling, well-wooded, apple-growing, dairying duchy on either side of the lower Seine, stretching westward to take in the fertile Côtentin peninsula. When we think of 'Normans', however, the image is of grim stone *donjons* and brutal mailed knights. The contrast forms one of the unresolved paradoxes of history. Perhaps we should reflect that Normandy, while rich enough to support the fierce military aristocracy implanted there by the Viking invasions, was yet not so rich that its people – especially its younger sons, trained for war from childhood – had no incentive to venture forth in search of land and fortune. The Norman expansion was merely part of a general outward migration from the provinces of the north-western Franks – northern Burgundy,

Lorraine, Flanders, Picardy, Normandy itself, Maine, Anjou, Poitou, and even Brittany, Celtic in speech and custom but politically dominated by the Norman duke. A trickle of men from these regions was perhaps beginning to enter Scotland before the death of Malcolm Canmore in 1093. His long reign of thirty-five years had seen a strengthening of Scottish links first with the Scandinavians of the far north (Malcolm's first queen was the widow of an earl of Orkney) and then, more significantly, with the Anglo-Saxon kingdom to the south.

It was in 1068 that extraordinary accidents of history had brought to the shores of Malcolm's kingdom as a political refugee, Edgar the Atheling ('heir'), the legitimate pretender to the English throne whose hopes had been dashed by the Norman conquest, and his sister Margaret. Although they had been born and brought up far away in Hungary and their experience of England had been confined to a few years, they represented in the eyes of countless Englishmen the prestige and the lawful succession of the old West Saxon dynasty. Soon after they had fled to Scotland King Malcolm married Margaret, as his second wife. This proved to be a momentous match, though not in terms of Anglo-French influence, for Margaret's Englishness was somewhat remote and there was almost nothing Norman or Frankish about her ancestry or background.

Queen Margaret was one of those meteoric characters of history who leave their mark regardless of patterns and trends. The fact that her marriage with Malcolm Canmore brought about an increase in Anglo-French influences in Scotland was mainly the accidental result of her ambition to rescue the Scots from what she considered to be their woeful ignorance and barbarity – not for nothing had she been brought up in Hungary in the generation after Saint Stephen had christianised the previously pagan Magyars. She herself was obviously regarded popularly as a saint long before her formal canonisation (1249). She provided that the main Forth ferry – the Queensferry as it was called in her honour – should be free for poor pilgrims, and she brought Benedictine monks, the first to be established in Scotland, from Canterbury to a new church at Dunfermline, which her youngest grandson King David I afterwards enlarged and promoted as Dunfermline Abbey. Margaret died in 1093 soon after hearing the news of her husband's death.

Almost as soon as King Malcolm and his Hungarian queen were dead, the Scots revolted against this foreign immigration (small-scale though it must surely have been), and would only allow Malcolm's heir, Duncan II, to keep the throne if he promised to introduce no more Normans or Englishmen to perform military service for him. Again one may see the close parallel with Ireland a century later, where Dermot Mac Murrough, king of Leinster, who had brought in the first Normans, was made – in vain – to promise not to bring in any more and to repatriate those he had brought as soon as possible. The anti-foreign reaction lasted for only three years. In 1097, Edgar, Duncan II's half-brother, gained the throne with the support of troops supplied by William Rufus, the Conqueror's son. Unmarried, Edgar was succeeded in turn by his two younger brothers Alexander I and David I. This re-markable span of sixty years during which the Crown was held by a single generation gave stability to Scottish royal government in a crucial period when powerful and rapacious Norman kings of England might well have been tempted to dismember or even swallow up the smaller and much weaker northern kingdom. Norman penetration of Scotland began in earnest in the time of the three brothers Edgar, Alexander and David. It became par-ticularly intensive under David I (1124–53), two whole generations after the Norman conquest of England. David held wide estates in the English midlands (the 'Honour of Huntingdon'), so that he had many ready-made Norman vassals, tenants by knight-service who would be glad of the chance to add to their lands and would expect to hold estates newly acquired in Scotland by the same military service which they were used to in England. This Norman penetration of Scotland took an outward and visible form about which we know a good deal. It also had a more inward, invisible effect which can hardly be traced at the time it was happening, but which can be seen through its ultimate results in medieval Scottish society.

The visible normanisation consisted of the settlement of powerful Anglo-Norman and Anglo-Breton and Anglo-Flemish barons, with their accompanying knights and servants, in the country between the Cheviots and the Clyde-Forth line, with a handful of outlyers in Fife and even in Moray, which fell into David I's direct possession in 1130. In Strathclyde and the south-west generally (save for Galloway and Nithsdale) David seems to have granted out existing territorial units of government or lord-ship, perhaps in some cases former petty principalities resembling the cantreds and commotes of Wales. In the east, in Lothian, Berwickshire, Tweeddale and Teviotdale, the incoming Normans seem to have been given smaller estates resembling more closely the manors of midland and northern England. The barons would hold their new lands by knight-service, and one of their first tasks would be to compel the inhabitants to build the earthwork and timber castles of the 'motte-and-bailey' type – 'motes' as the Scots soon learned to call them and still would if the Ordnance Survey and archaeologists had not taught them overwise. One of the most splendid examples in southern Scotland is the great Mote of Urr (Kirkcudbrightshire), built probably for Walter of Berkeley, chamberlain to King William the Lion, not long after 1165. More typically these motes were fairly small structures, shaped like Christmas puddings, scores of which may still be seen, scattered widely across the Scottish countryside, especially in the south. Good examples, close to main roads, are on the golf course at Carnwath in Lanarkshire (a castle of the de Somervilles since David I's time), at Duffus in Moray (surmounted by a later stone tower), and at Inverurie, at the confluence of Urie and Don, where King William the Lion's brother David built the 'Bass of Inverurie' as his motte castle probably in the 1180s.

In southern Scotland before 1153 the pattern of Norman settle-ment was thus mainly determined by grants from the king of sizeable blocks of royal demesne in favour of military vassals most of whom came from the Scottish king's English lands. Robert de Brus (Bruce) was given Annandale for ten knights' service, Ranulf de Sules (Soulis) Liddesdale, Hugh de Morville – King David's constable – Cunningham and Lauderdale, Robert Avenel Eskdale. These families came originally from western Normandy, had benefited in a small way from the Norman conquest of England, and now gained much more land and power as 're-exports' to Scotland. Brix (whence Bruce) and Morville are near Cherbourg, Soulles (whence Soulis) is near St Lô. Some other famous families introduced under David I clearly had a Norman origin, but it is not always easy to give them a location south of the Channel. One family prominent on the Honour of Huntingdon had already, by the early twelfth century, taken its surname of Lindsey – Lindsay – from the largest division of Lincolnshire where they were lords, under the earls of Chester, of the rich manor of Fordington. Lindsay is thus an English name, but the family's earliest known forenames, Baldric, Walter, William and Drogo, point unmistakably to a Norman origin, at least on the paternal side.

Men from far afield, with no ties of tenure, were also drawn to Scotland by King David's generous patronage. From Shropshire, for example, came Walter, younger son of a Breton named Alan son of Flaald who had been highly favoured by Henry I. Walter son of Alan joined King David's service about 1136 and was made steward – chief officer of the household. He was also given the lordships of Renfrew and North Kyle (Walter's Kyle) in Ayrshire. It was probably also the king who arranged a marriage for Walter with a lady named Eschina of London. Doubtless Eschina was a 'Norman' on her father's side, but through her mother she was apparently the granddaughter of a member of the ancient Northumbrian aristocracy of the border country, Uhtred son of Liulf lord of Mow. Walter and Eschina were ancestors of the Stewarts, a long and still continuing line : their direct descendant in the sixth generation took the Scottish throne in 1371 as King Robert II. Walter himself was typical enough of the continental settlers of good family who were favoured by David I : not in fact Norman, but the younger son of a man who had acquired lands in several parts of England in the wake of the Norman conquest. And of course Walter brought with him in his train a whole group of followers, knights, esquires, serjeants, archers and household servants, with their womenfolk, many of whom settled on lands provided by their lord in what later became the counties of Ayr and Renfrew. Among them was one Richard Wallace (*Walensis*, 'the Welshman'), a castle-garrison serjeant in Shropshire, who has probably left his Christian name in the Ayrshire parish of Riccarton, 'Richard's village'. We shall never know whether Richard's family were called 'Welsh' because, though Normans, they lived among the Welsh in Shropshire, or because they really were Welsh but had adopted the Anglo-Norman way of life. The Wallaces prospered in the great Stewart fief of south-west Scotland, and William Wallace, a younger son of a cadet branch of the family established at Elderslie in Paisley, has given the surname an immortality equal to that of the Stewarts themselves. Even the grandfather of Walter son of Alan, the dimly obscure Flaald from

Dol in Brittany, has won his own kind of immortality as the equally dim Fleance of Shakespeare's *Macbeth*.

The beginnings of the great Scottish house of Stewart may be seen as a microcosm of the whole era of Norman settlement and colonisation in Scotland. The king grants high office and rich lands to the head of the new family, who in turn settles his followers in lesser fiefs, many to be held by military service. As part of the process castles are built, religious houses and hospitals are founded and endowed, parish churches established or enriched, and trading towns or 'burghs' are planted and given the necessary municipal and trading privileges. All of this can be seen going forward in the time of the first Stewart, Walter son of Alan (*c.* 1136–1177) and his son and successor Alan (1177–1204). Walter built – or received from the king – the first castle of Renfrew, and probably built another at Dundonald. Paisley Priory – afterwards Abbey – was founded in 1163 for Cluniac monks from Much Wenlock in Shropshire, chiefly in honour of Saint James the Great whose shrine at Compostella was then approaching the height of its renown. (It was only later that the ancient local cult of Saint Mirren of Paisley re-asserted itself). Walter also founded a hospital for lepers at Morriston in Berwickshire and contributed to the endowments of St Peter's Hospital in York, as well as to famous Scottish abbeys of royal foundation at Kelso and Melrose. His son and grandson, Alan and Walter II, continued these benefactions and made other gifts to monasteries and churches further afield – Coupar Angus Abbey, Canterbury Cathedral (in honour of Thomas the Martyr) and the well-known pilgrimage church of the Holy Rood at Bromholm in Norfolk, whose mother-house at Castle Acre had been befriended by their forebear Alan son of Flaald. As for towns, Renfrew began as a royal burgh and after passing into the Stewart's possession may have been rather overshadowed by Rutherglen and Glasgow. Nevertheless, it seems to have enjoyed a modest prosperity, and the same is true of the family's other burgh, Prestwick in Ayrshire, which kept its ancient constitution for many centuries. Of the towns which grew up on the Stewarts' estates, it seems likely that Paisley flourished most vigorously from an early date, but rather surprisingly it did not become a burgh until 1488.

If this first phase of 'Norman' settlement in Scotland, always and rightly associated with David I, had been the whole story, we should still have to recognise it as a formative influence on our history. It had, after all, familiarised the Scots with the feudal system of landholding which is still the basis of Scottish land law; it had brought new forms of government by means of royal castles and burghs, sheriffs, justiciars and knight-service baronies; it had established contacts between Scotland and the latest currents of intellectual and religious life pervading western Christendom in the twelfth century; it had, above all, given added strength and a new direction to the ancient Scottish kingship and thus in a real sense created, or at least made possible, the medieval Scottish kingdom which endured till 1638 despite the shock of Flodden and the strains set up by the Reformation and the union of the Scottish and English crowns in 1603.

But when King David died, an old man, at Carlisle in May, 1153, a second and even more thoroughgoing phase of Anglo-French influence was yet to come. From 1153 to 1214 the throne was held by two of David's grandsons, Malcolm the Maiden and William the Lion. Unlike their grandfather, who had no Norman blood, Malcolm and William were the sons of a Norman mother, Ada de Varenne, herself descended from a Capetian king of France. They were strongly imbued with the prevailing ideals of the Frankish world to which they were obviously proud to belong. This was a world of professionalised knightly warfare, of chivalry, of courtly love and *chansons de geste*. It was also a world in which a passionate and often tender Christian faith could sometimes be qualified by an uncertainty as to whether Christ was inspiring raw barbarian warriors to find room in their hearts for Christian love, for compassion towards the poor and the sick and protectiveness towards women and children, or whether, on the contrary, Christ was being enlisted within an order of knighthood which for all its Christian invocations displayed strong features of Germanic paganism.

It was not just that Anglo-French influences were intensified under these francophile rulers. They were also spread much more widely across the Scottish kingdom. Knights' fees were created in Galloway and Nithsdale (untouched by David I), and, with more permanent effect, north of the Forth, in Fife and Gowrie, in Angus and Mearns, in Aberdeenshire and Moray, and even as far north as Sutherland. Settlers were encouraged to come not only from the English estates of the Scottish kings (a reservoir which may have begun to dry up), but also direct from Normandy, from over-populated Flanders, and from almost every part of England, especially Northumberland, Yorkshire, the Welsh borders and Somerset. Under Malcolm IV's direction Clydesdale was feudalised with a colony of Flemish adventurers who have given their personal names to such places as Houston, Thankerton, Symington, Wiston, Lamington, Roberton – as well as to places not in the Clyde valley such as Symington in Ayrshire and Lockerbie in Dumfriesshire. One notable family originating in French Flanders, in the region of Béthune, was that of de Quincy. Robert de Quincy first came to Scotland at the end of Malcolm IV's reign. By the time his grandson Roger had died in 1264, the last male representative of the main line of the family, the de Quincys had acquired vast estates in many parts of Scotland, the hereditary constableship, and an English earldom. And even though the de Quincys themselves may have left little or no trace on Scottish society, many of the descendants of the men they brought with them – e.g. the Beatons and Béthunes whose ancestor was one Robert de Béthune, an original companion of Robert de Quincy – must be living in Scotland today or will have gone to form part of the Scottish component in areas of British settlement scattered across the world.

A brief list will show how many famous Scottish surnames would be missing if King Malcolm and King William had not pursued the same policy as their grandfather and with even more vigour. Agnew, Hay, Moubray, Sinclair, Ramsay, Boswell, Landells, Bisset, Menzies, Lovel, Barclay (Berkeley), Vallance (Valognes), Montgomery, Colville, Fraser, Gourlay, Grant, Carvel – these and many others have become thoroughly acclimatised and naturalised in Scotland since the first bearer of the name got a toe-hold north of the Border through the favour of our two 'normanising' kings, of whom a near contemporary said, wrongly and rather unfairly, that 'they held only Frenchmen dear and would never love their own people'. Some families seem to have become naturalised very quickly indeed, so that it is not always easy to trace their continental origin. At first glance it is impossible to see behind the homely Perthshire name of Muschet the Norman village of Montfiquet, near Bayeux, from which came Richard de Montfiquet, the first of the Scots Muschets. Sometimes a Norman surname might be dropped altogether, although this was rare, for the

Normans seem to have been proud of their surnames. Two of William the Lion's most prominent knights belonged to a family named de la Kernelle, who must have come from La Carneille near Argentan. While junior branches of the family kept the surname until it emerged as Carvel or Carvill, the senior line, holding the knight's fee of Guthrie in Angus, seem to have taken the name of Guthrie from their lands at an early date. There are several instances where greater families brought lesser ones in their train and yet it has turned out to be the lesser family which has survived and prospered while the greater has dwindled or been extinguished. Thus the de Soules family brought the first Hays and Agnews; the Bissets brought the Grants; and the long extinct family of de Normanville brought the family of de Mesnières or de Meyners, which we now call Menzies. The most startling example of rise and fall is of course provided by the great family of Cumin, Comyn or Cumming. Their Scottish career began when King David I arranged a good match for Richard Cumin, nephew of his chancellor William Cumin (certainly a Norman, but of quite humble origins). By the middle of the thirteenth century the Comyns had become the most powerful baronial clan in Scotland, with enormous estates in Galloway, the Borders, Aberdeenshire and the Highlands, two or three earldoms and a guaranteed place in the king's councils. A hundred years later, mainly because of the family's opposition to Robert the Bruce, there was little left of all this Comyn empire save for the Cummings of Altyre (Moray) and the Cumines of Rattray (Aberdeenshire) who have carried on the family name down to the present.

It would be wrong to think of the age of Anglo-French influence in Scottish history as nothing but a matter of family trees and clan pedigrees, fascinating though these have always been to all Scots. The structure of Scottish government in the middle ages was a unique amalgam, not yet fully explored or understood, in which very diverse elements, Celtic, English, Scandinavian and Frankish, were compounded – in precisely what proportions it may never be possible to determine. But it would be absurd to deny or under-estimate the value and importance of the Frankish or French contribution. The feudalism of Scotland was Norman or Anglo-Norman and the knights' fees and motes had their counterpart in the Scottish setting of some of the Norman-French poetic romances, and in the confident way in which they new settlers renamed Edinburgh Tanebroc or (more romantically, after the Arthurian stories which they had been delighted to adopt) Le Chastel des Pucelles, the 'Maidens' Castle'; Dumbarton 'Chastel de Dounbretaigne'; Roxburgh Castle 'le Marche Mont' (Marchmont); even Carstairs 'Chastel Tarres'. The royal household, at the heart of government, was French in conception: the king attended by his Steward, Chancellor, Chamberlain, Butler, Constable and Marischal, while in the country at large the king's justice was administered by justiciars, a characteristically Norman institution. When Frenchmen began to settle in Scotland in significant numbers, around 1100, they found a king, unanointed and uncrowned, mormaers only slowly becoming earls, clan chiefs called toshachs, a ministerial lesser nobility of thanes (here and there identified with toshachs), hereditary dempsters or judges, secularised abbots and other clergy, and a social organisation which was at least partly tribal. This pattern was not changed, still less abolished, overnight. But its archaic Celtic and Anglo-Celtic character was far less prominent by the later thirteenth century than it had been at the start of the twelfth, and the most powerful solvent in the whole process of change was the presence of ideas brought directly or indirectly from the continent, especially from the Frankish territories of northern France.

Nowhere was this more striking than in the Church. The very first of the orders of 'reformed' Benedictine monachism to cross the Channel were the monks from Thiron, near Chartres, who came in 1113 to Selkirk and moved fifteen years later to establish their great abbey at Kelso. The Cistercians came to Melrose as early as 1136, while the order was still under the direct influence of Saint Bernard. The Augustinian canons of Cambuskenneth abbey (1140) came from Arrouaise in Picardy, those of Jedburgh abbey (c. 1138) probably from Beauvais, while the monks who set up the priories of Beauly west of Inverness and Pluscardine near Elgin, about 1230, came from the remote house of Val des Choux founded in the forest north of Dijon at the end of the twelfth century, and belonged to an order which had daughter-houses only in France and Scotland. The secular clergy also were much influenced by new blood and new brooms from the south. A recognisable diocesan organisation was established and in 1192 brought into immediate dependence upon the papacy. Dozens and scores of parishes were created, and in many cases must have

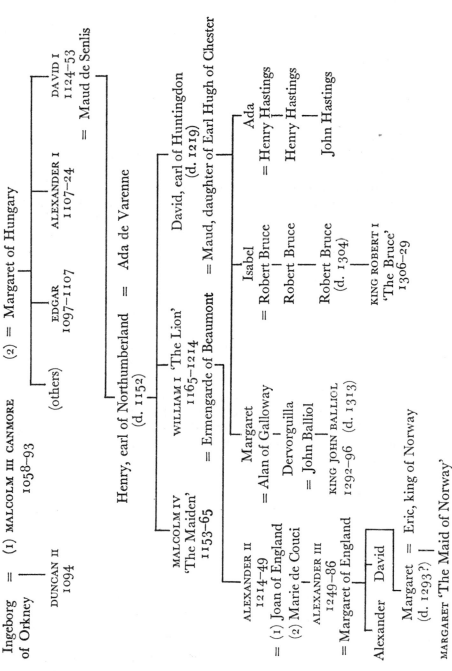

been provided with small stone churches of which so few still remain : Leuchars in Fife and Dalmeny in West Lothian being among the best of the handful of survivors. For a century from *c.* 1130 Anglo-Norman or French bishops predominated in the Scottish church, and one of the last of them, William Malvoisin, from the district of Mantes near Paris, ruled the principal Scottish see, St Andrews, from 1202 to 1238, and probably did more for the unity, discipline and *morale* of the church of Scotland than any other single bishop of the twelfth or thirteenth centuries.

Anglo-French influences did not make Scotland either an English or a French country, nor the Scots an English or a French nation. They permeated deeply and permanently, so that the Scotland which successfully resisted the onslaught of Edward I and his son was a very different country from that on whose shores Margaret of Hungary, afterwards Saint Margaret, had landed as a refugee in 1068. Yet the inhabitants of Scotland must have retained a basic continuity, and could reject as well as absorb if it suited them. In 1163 Walter, the first Stewart, granted his monks of Paisley Abbey a tenth of the venison from the hinds and does taken locally in what his charter calls *fermeisun*, i.e. the close season (French, *fermer*) after November 11th, when stags are protected but hinds are not. By the later middle ages the monks of Paisley, blithely misreading their founder's charter, were referring to their estates of 'Ferrenes', and today the Fereneze Hills above Barrhead are a reminder of the fact that all influences in history reach, eventually, the point of exhaustion.

CHAPTER X

The Making of Scotland
A. A. M. Duncan

On 15 June, 1215, when John, King of England, was among recalcitrant barons at Runnymede, somewhere in Scotland the young king Alexander II – the 'red fox', King John called him – received a welcome gift from one of his barons. For on the death of his father, the aged King William, his enemies had 'entered Moray, namely Donald bán the son of MacWilliam and Kenneth mac Heth, and the son of a certain king of Ireland, with a numerous band of evildoers. MacTaggart attacked them and mightily overthrew the king's enemies and cut off their heads and presented them as new gifts to the new king. . . And because of this the lord king made him a new knight'. The families of Mac-William and MacHeth, with a claim the one to the throne, the other to the earldom of Moray, had been thorns in the flesh of the Scottish kings for almost a century, representing the faded vision of a kingdom with strong provincial loyalties, pre-eminently Celtic in language and institutions but nonetheless held and exploited with its dependent Anglo-Saxon provinces south of the Forth by the warrior kings of the royal dynasty – the only kingdom of size and significance in the otherwise fragmented Celtic world.

This eleventh-century promise had faltered and failed as the twelfth century kings accepted men from England and France into their service and friendship and French language and culture, pre-eminent throughout Western Europe, into their court. The achievements of this band of incomers discussed in the previous chapter were out of all proportion to their numbers because their way of life was adopted enthusiastically by the native aristocracy everywhere save in the far north. Moray and Ross had yielded consistent support to the dissident MacWilliam and MacHeth families, invading presumably from Ireland, but in the 1180s these rebels had been suppressed with the aid of the men of Galloway under their lord, baptised Lachlan but calling himself by the French euphonym Roland.

About 1210 William Comyn was favoured by the king with the heiress of Buchan as wife and the title of earl, this in time to provide a valuable contingent against the rebels in Moray. In 1228 his son was similarly active and was rewarded with a great lordship in Badenoch and Lochaber with control of Strathspey which had proved a route for the king's enemies as well as his avenging armies. This senior branch, the Red Comyns (from their heraldic colour, while the earls of Buchan, a junior line, were the Black Comyns) established themselves in the mote at Ruthven near Kingussie, and in the second half of the century built the simple stone castles of Lochindorb and Inverlochy and even intruded themselves into Athol, where, much to the annoyance of the earl, they built a castle at Blair. In this way the Grampian massif was, if not controlled, then at least policed, for the king of Scots.

'Celtic' risings continued until the 1230s but that of 1215 with which we began was the last of importance and it was suppressed by a Celtic aristocrat of Ross, MacTaggart – 'son of the priest' – lord of the ancient but laicised Celtic monastery of Applecross. The king who had found the native earls of Dunbar, Fife, Strathearn and of the other southerly provinces apt for assimilation to Anglo-French culture now found himself a more strongly Celtic agent in the home of resistance. His reward was to be made a 'new knight', token of acceptance into the social order of French speaking chivalry. A few years later the title earl of Ross was conferred upon him, while that of earl of Sutherland was given to a junior branch of the family of Flemish origin which had settled in Moray about 1150 and had taken Moray to be its name. These new earls enjoyed an independence of action attributable to remoteness from the wealthy lowland zone where the king generally resided. Yet when in 1222 the men of Caithness burned their bishop for his insistence upon his tenth penny it was the king who led an army to kill the ring-leaders, cut hand and foot from eighty bystanders and fine the whole deliquent community. For this offence against God's servant endangered the standing of the whole kingdom and the immortal soul of its king; if he wished, his hand could fall heavily in redemptive punishment upon any part of his realm, however remote.

Or almost so. Only in Argyll had the native aristocracy seemed immune from royal control, while the western isles were part of the Norwegian not the Scottish kingdom. In forty-five years from 1221 to 1266 both passed to Scotland. In 1221–22 the Clyde basin and in 1249 Mid-Argyll and Lorn were subdued by naval expeditions. From 1244 the king's aim was to recover the Isles from Norway but because of a royal minority (1249–61) the campaign was postponed till 1262 when the Scots invaded Skye from Ross. The Norwegian king's retaliatory expedition in 1263 with its indecisive skirmish at Largs merely made the Scots more determined and by 1265 only the Outer Isles were unconquered; the Norse surrendered them by the treaty of Perth in 1266.

Late in the thirteenth century a map-maker seeking to draw out the 'kingdom of Scotland' would have shown its bounds from Tweed (including Berwick) to Solway, a southerly dip to include Man, the whole mainland and western isles to the Pentland Firth, but not beyond to the Northern Isles. The Isle of Man passed to England from 1296, and Berwick in effect from the same date; the Northern Isles became Scottish in 1468–69 but gradually lost their Norse speech from the fourteenth century to the seventeenth. But although all would have agreed that this was the kingdom, our map-maker might well have looked puzzled if we had commented on the inclusion of Man in 'Scotland.'

In the twelfth and earlier centuries Scotland, *Scotia*, was the land north of the Forth, while to the south lay Lothian on the east coast and Cumbria (alias Strathclyde) on the west. The kingdom took its name from that part which had extended its rule over the rest and 'kingdom of Scotland' certainly included all three parts. But only in the thirteenth century had Scotland, *Scotia*, come to mean not only the lesser part but also the whole land (and in some spheres the older usage lingered on into the fourteenth century). Moreover if David I and his successors were 'king of Scots', they had inherited this use of 'Scots' from a much earlier age when it meant the men of *Scotia*; writing of 1216 the Melrose chronicler speaks of Alexander II invading England from Scotland 'with his whole army excepting the Scots from whom he took money' (in place of army service) and of 1217 he speaks even more clearly of 'a general army, namely of English, Scots and Galwegians', where the English are the men of Lothian. The English certainly did not distinguish in this way – all were Scots – and this limited usage of 'Scots' was perhaps becoming old fashioned. But it is striking how among the many citations of barons, greater men, good men, or army, 'of Scotland' there are to be found so few Scottish examples of 'Scot' or 'Scots' before the troubled times of the 1290s. Men sensed first of all a king

I

and kingdom, and secondly a land, Scotland, because these could be seen and they had a function in at least the politics of the time. But why unite in one abstraction a wide diversity of languages and ways of life by speaking of the inhabitants of Scotland as 'Scots'? What function did they have in common except obedience? It is not fortuitous that they appear regularly in only one phrase, and in second place there: king of Scots.

One group which had much in common was the wealthy landowners whose cultural affinities were expressed in the building of castles. In the Lowland zone which includes the central belt but also stretches up the east coast, along the Moray Firth and as far north as Dornoch, different styles were employed according to the taste and resources of the builders. At Kildrummy the earl of Mar, at Dirleton the de Vaux, and at Bothwell the Morays, favoured a strong round donjon with walls of enormous thickness; elsewhere the castle of enceinte, a curtain wall with a large stone gatehouse enclosing a courtyard with (vanished) wooden buildings was perhaps more general than surviving examples (e.g. Inverlochy, Lochindorb, Mugdock) would suggest. But at least equally numerous is the residence of much more obviously peaceful character, the hall-house, a two or three storey stone house with windows and no strong military features (e.g. Rait, Morton). Now although industrialisation has removed many buildings of these kinds, we have recently come to recognise an increasing number of them, clearly attributable to the thirteenth century. Castles in the north are documented in Easter Ross and Easter Sutherland; in the west they are found in mainland Kintyre, Argyll, Lismore and Mull. From Dunaverty at the Mull of Kintyre to the hall-house at Aros on Mull, and including such a masterpiece as Dunstaffnage and such remote strongholds as Tioram and Mingarry, Argyll is now recognised as a province whose leaders fully deserved their contemporary description of 'barons' as well as the modern one of 'chiefs'. They knew how to demand, and get, the best in prestigious housing and were in no cultural or political backwater. Yet beyond Ardnamurchan point, in Tiree, the small Isles, the Outer Isles, in Skye and on the long ragged coast from Castle Tioram northward, there is no sight of such buildings. There are monasteries in Argyll, but none in the north-west; many recognisable early church buildings in Argyll but few if any beyond it. All of which shows that at the highest social level Argyll was part of Scotland in a real sense while the outermost northern and north-western fringe was not. But this common culture was found only at the highest social level. The men of Argyll doubtless retained the pre-eminent social functions of the kindred and its head in the same way as the men of Galloway whose insistence upon their 'liberties' and upon the 'law of Galloway' lasted well into the fourteenth century, resisting the castles, sheriffs and juries foisted on them by the king after the unified lordship of Galloway broke up in 1234. Nonetheless the Gaidhealtachd was split into those in Buchan, Strathspey, Athol, Argyll and Galloway whose lords accepted the ways of Lowland Scotland, and those beyond who knew them not. Among the latter Gaelic speech and Norse-derived place names are still strong; among the former English speech and Gaelic-derived place names are general. In such ways we betray our forbears.

Moreover, the modern eye which discerns the strength of the castles of the landowning class may mislead the imagination into a notion of 'feudal anarchy'. In fact, as the hall-house suggests, thirteenth century society was remarkably peaceful. Of royal castles we know most and can recognise that they were built as safe storehouses for wealth and produce, and as intermittent residences often sited for the king's hunting. Men were called to garrison them in time of crisis and the king's agents rode in and out upon his business, but for much of the year their only full-time resident was the castle janitor. Before Scottish independence was compromised in 1291 two crises shook the otherwise peaceful, even sedate, political life of Scotland which these castles ensured. One was a struggle for power among barons during the minority of Alexander III (1249–61) which reveals the existence of those cliques and ambitions which trouble any government when its controlling head, whether thirteenth century king or modern president, is unable to rule. The immense power of the Comyns under the late king cast them in the role first of reformers of the state (dominated by the ambitious Alan Durward), then of a closed oligarchy swept away in its turn by leading magnates of moderate views. Striking, however, is the reliance of both the Comyns and their opponents upon the help of the English king in bringing about their palace revolutions; to all he was a man to be trusted, with a disinterested concern for a peaceful Scottish kingdom so long as it made no alliance with France. And broadly this Scottish judgment was justified. Yet when Alexander III (who had, we might say, a vested interest in separateness) took over government he is found pursuing a policy of greater independence, buying out an English family which had inherited the Constableship and a monastery with English ties. Some English landowners retained major Scottish interests but by the late thirteenth century almost all Scottish barons were conscious of their overriding allegiance to the Scottish king, and the strong tide of Anglo-French cultural influence was on the ebb. Unfortunately among the exceptions were two English barons, holders of wide Scottish estates, Balliol and Bruce (grandfather of King Robert I), upon whom in 1286 and more clearly in 1290, devolved the right to the Scottish throne. These men were almost certainly to blame for selling out the kingdom's independence to Edward I in 1291, but they did so after Bruce had caused years of crisis (1286–90) in which the Scottish barons had again showed themselves trusting of the good intentions of the English king in holding him in check. The treaty which they negotiated, if carried into effect, would have anticipated the union of 1603 by uniting two kingships in the person of one king who would have lived in England.

But the ruling caste in Scotland was no longer French in manners and customs as it had been in 1200. The French romance about his ancestor commissioned by Alan lord of Galloway before 1234 had no successors and there is scant evidence of what the aristocracy read. One or two pointers may be significant : there was a recrudescence of interest in the Celtic past, so that an earl of Fife could give the surname Macduff as a forename to his son : showing the interest in things Celtic (and the incomprehension!) of an essentially non-Celtic people. And there was no use in documents of French. In English government and baronial life French was the language of communication but the Scots employed it only to write to England – except for Bruce who thus again betrays his English loyalty. We reason that most Scottish magnates by the late thirteenth century preferred to speak not French but that northern English known as Scots and thereby strengthened social bonds with their English speaking dependent lairds as well as political understanding with England.

The causes of this change were doubtless complex. Yet undoubtedly of great importance was the commercial and urban development sustained by the great European boom of the twelfth and thirteenth century. Expanded population, consumption and production demanded an efficient means of exchange and offered rich profits to any state which exploited its opportunities. Urban privileges were given from the time of David I and a policy of encouraging foreign settlement in the towns was so successful that from Berwick to Inverness or even Dingwall the English tongue filled their streets. Perth, situated at a river crossing and also at the place where the Tay becomes tidal and thus accessible to small sea-going vessels, was at a nodal point of communications. The original town may have lain between the castle and the kirk. But at some time, presumably in the twelfth century, a larger scheme was laid out and Perth became the most important town in Scotland after Berwick. Its institutions like those of other Scottish burghs had English names; the main thoroughfares were known as 'gaits', something to 'gang' along. Like other Scottish towns Perth had a provost, a royal agent, at its head. At Berwick, however, the town grew so prosperous on the wool trade to Flanders that the king (doubtless for a reward) allowed its merchant gild to take over burgh government and Berwick the 'Alexandria of the north', alone of Scottish towns had a mayor, the 'great man' of the gild at its head. Yet because seafaring techniques were rudimentary most European trade was still coastbound, while the great centres of population and markets lay to the south of Scotland. Both these factors effectively bound Scottish trade to use English waters and ports and Scottish commerce was to a large extent an extension of English trade – which strengthened the already pronounced English character of Scottish town life.

Townsfolk were few but their influence great, for they were opportunity to any with a need to buy or sell. They took with them the language of commerce, English, into all their dealings. In Lothian they would find that all spoke English but in Fife, Angus and Gowrie the language of business gradually ousted the languages of the aristocrat, French, and the peasant, Gaelic. By what stages this happened is obscure but the struggle between the two principal native vernaculars, Scots and Gaelic, was resolved in victory for the former and by the end of the thirteenth century Gaelic speech outside the Highland line was probably limited largely to Galloway and Buchan. We can be as sure as of anything in our history that William Wallace and most of his men ordinarily spoke Scots. And if our map is to express the personality of Scotland this is another characterisation that must appear upon it : there was a Gaidhealtachd which was a little larger than the

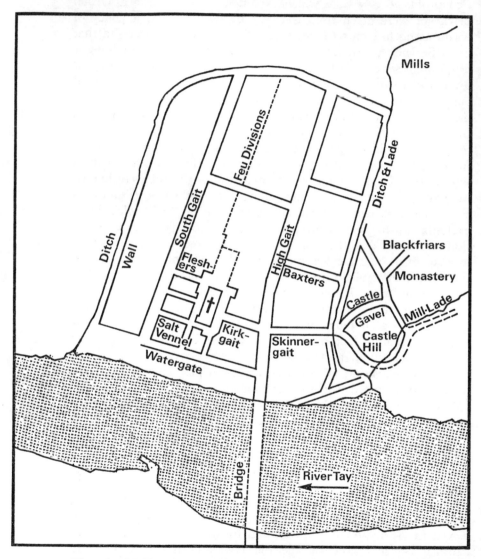

Fig 16 Medieval Perth (The bridge was built before 1220 to replace a ford. The straight line of the Feu Divisions suggests that the two main streets were laid out at the same time)

Highlands and much larger than the outermost north-western fringe which escaped Anglo-French influences. Yet it was shrinking.

Perhaps because Gaelic was still widespread enough to be spoken by some with a Lowland way of life, contemporaries offer few comments upon distinctions of speech. There seems to have been little of that Anglo-Saxon hostility towards Celtic speech as sheer perverseness best corrected by unsparing chastisement, which has been prevalent since the fifteenth century. What they do speak of are social and legal distinctions within society between free and unfree. Sales of 'native men' have survived in numbers from the early and mid thirteenth centuries; these were men unable to leave the status, duties and obligations to their lords into which they had been born. In the twelfth century pursuit of the fugitive 'native' is common enough to show that he was a real asset to his lord. He, his wife and children must work on the land and pay rent at the will of the lord who was free to sell them to another and refuse to sell to them the freedom which they might offer to buy. Yet if this is the theory to which legal documents subscribe, it is doubtful that it remained the fact as the thirteenth century progressed. It is dangerous to generalise for geography imposed many variations. Change was most rapid near the ready markets of the larger towns, and remote areas were probably very conservative. Moreover so limited were the means of communication that regional variation could be drastic. Rains washing out a harvest would raise the cost of the winter loaf but poor roads and carts prevented the law of supply and demand from operating to relieve famine, which must often have caused a heavy mortality. Yet the overwhelming impression given by the sources is one of economic prosperity and social mobility.

Certainly by the end of the thirteenth century it was the land they held (and not their birth) which imposed servitudes upon many peasants. In Lothian, where we are best informed, these servitudes were limited to mowing and harvest works; the rest had been compounded into the payment of rent. Moreover there was wide variation in the economic position of individual peasants, from the husbandmen with a hundred or more acres each down to the poorest cottager without even a garden, and the wage labourer hiring himself out to other more fortunate peasants. So far as the lord (lay aristocrat or ecclesiastic) to whom their rents came was concerned, such peasants may have been unfree, subject to his will in his court, but the reality of the lord's power was surely economic rather than legal. Both lord and peasant wished to maximise their returns from the land which the latter held of the former, which meant frequent adjustments of rent and changes of tenancy, not rigid holdings and unwanted labours. It meant that the richer peasant (whose tenure was still insecure) must guard his precious gains in a harshly competitive society and an environment where nature is notoriously unsmiling. The poorest peasant must die under the dike in winter's cold after a bad autumn's rain. And those between must make shift as best they could to meet the lord's demands in rent, for if they failed there was assuredly another willing to take their cottar house and land.

This was no static society of the old-fashioned picture-book Middle Ages. Population grew and with it pressure on resources. The lord's share of the village field shrank as his peasants' ploughs took over more and more to fatten the lord's rent book. New land was broken out, much of it marginally productive. Great flocks of sheep grazed hill pastures and profits from their wool financed castle and monastery building. The rich were almost certainly getting richer; many middling families were able to make satisfactory provision for younger sons – that is, they too were in real terms better off though some certainly went to the wall. Among the peasantry too economic distinctions were perhaps accentuated so that the rich peasant and poor laird were indistinguishable. These consequences of two centuries of economic expansion, of lively demand for bread and cloth, produced a society which even in Scotland had stretched its resources to the limits imposed by its technology. But in the process legal servitude (which may have meant slavery even as late as the eleventh century) had shrunk from serfdom inherited in the blood to unfree tenures with modest obligations on the holder. The last we hear of personal unfreedom in medieval Scotland is in Moray in 1364 but on the eve of the war of independence in the 1290s it was already much diminished.

On 27 April 1296 at Dunbar a two-century long phase in the history of Scotland came to an end with the defeat of its aristocratic leaders in battle, the subsequent abdication of their king John (Balliol), and the imposition of direct English rule under Edward I. For a decade the barons had struggled with the unfamiliar problems of government and the vexed one of settlement of the royal succession. In 1290 they had agreed to a union of the Scottish and English kingships by marriage but had stipulated that the kingdom was to remain distinct : Scots were to hold the great offices of state, and they were not to have to go for law or administrative act outside the bounds of the kingdom.

These terms are revealing. They show that these men thought not of a nation of Scots but of a kingdom, of a territory whose magnates were bound in allegiance to a common king. Their last king had defended the independence of the kingdom because independence was personified in his own position. But those bound in allegiance to him had no such vested interest. With an absentee king their interest was in protecting or even increasing their own influence in decision-making processes by retaining them in the kingdom. In 1249–59 the barons had compromised the king's position while jockeying for power with English help, and in 1290 they abandoned the king's position while seeking to protect their own. They were not successful in doing so and in 1296, again setting aside the king (this time because he was too weak), they took up arms in defence of the right to do the kingdom's business within the kingdom. These words are perhaps too harsh a description of the unconscious attitudes of honest men trying to do their best in the unfamiliar role of interim rulers with a responsibility for the kingdom in wardship. Great lords in Buchan, Fife or Kyle where their social prestige and royally-conferred offices made them unquestioned leaders, they were regarded by all as *the* community of the kingdom. This indeed is what they called themselves – not the Scots, but the community of the realm, and it was this community and the whole tradition of a baronial political class which went down to failure at Dunbar.

Economic strength had long been more widely spread among other landowners – great and small lairds, freeholders and even rich peasants. So long as king and baronage ruled effectively they had no political claims. Now all was changed for the English garrisoned Scotland, threatening taxation and military call-up as well as practising extortion and bad debts. Unlike the baronage these classes knew nothing of the English king, had no lands in England and no acquaintance with overwhelming English resources. But they knew from long habits of obedience that they were of Scotland and they too now laid claim to be part of the community of the realm. They sustained through many vicissitudes, a struggle against the English in which the word 'freedom' recurs ever more insistently. This is not to deny that the aristocracy played a significant part nor to suggest that anything democratic was born in these years. The politically significant increased from a few tens of barons to a few hundred of knights. A few thousand freeholders and husbandmen were active in the army and so achieved military importance. But the condition of most men changed slowly and (to them) imperceptibly; doubtless a deep pool of peasant ignorance and indifference remained undisturbed in many areas. Yet enough had changed. Two centuries of growing wealth and able and effective kings had created Scotland, the notion of a kingdom which, however disparate its languages and cultures in different regions and at different social levels, was nonetheless bound in allegiance to one king. A few years of political blundering and the risings of William Wallace, Andrew Moray and Robert Bruce, the king, demanded action from hitherto silent social groups. Their war was conducted with cries about the nation race and people of Scots which at least in intensity had no precedent and which must reflect popular beliefs and slogans. 'Nation' stressed their birth in the kingdom, 'race' their descent within the kingdom, and 'people' their social comprehensiveness in the kingdom; but all these words were (and strictly still should) be used of a people not of a land. By invoking in these three words their standing to act, they also created, for the kingdom, the Scots.

Books for further reading

Chapters *1* and *2*

FEACHEM, R. *A guide to prehistoric Scotland* Batsford, 1963.
HENSHALL, A. S. *The chambered tombs of Scotland* Edinburgh University P., vol. I 1964. vol. II due 1972.
PIGGOTT, S. *Ancient Europe: a survey* Edinburgh University P., 1965.
PIGGOTT, S. *The Neolithic cultures of the British Isles* C.U.P., 1954.
PIGGOTT, S. ed. *The prehistoric peoples of Scotland* Routledge & K. Paul, 1962.
RIVET, A. L. F. ed. *The Iron Age in Northern Britain* Edinburgh University P., 1967. op.
ROSS, A. *Everyday life of the Pagan Celts* Batsford, 1970.

Chapter *3*

BURN, A. R. *Agricola and Roman Britain* English Universities P., 1953. op.
MACDONALD, Sir George *The Roman wall in Scotland* O.U.P., 2nd. ed. 1934. op.
RICHMOND, Sir Ian ed. *Roman and native in North Britain* Nelson, 1958. op.
ROBERTSON, A. S. *The Antonine wall* Glasgow Archaeological Society, 1970. Rev. ed. 1968. T. & A. Constable.
TACITUS *The Agricola and the Germania* trans. H. Mattingley and S. A. Handford. Penguin Books, 1970.

Chapters *4, 5, 6* and *7*

ADOMNAN *Life of Columba* edited by A. O. and M. O. Anderson. Nelson, 1961. op.
ANDERSON, A. O. ed. *Early sources of Scottish history, vol. I* Oliver & Boyd, 1922. op.
ANEIRIN *The Gododdin: the oldest Scottish poem* ed. by K. H. Jackson. Edinburgh University P., 1969.

BEDE *Ecclesiastical history of the English people* ed. by B. Colgrave and R. A. B. Mynors. O.U.P., 1970

CHADWICK, H. M. *Early Scotland* C.U.P., 1949. op.

CRUDEN, S. H. *The early Christian and Pictish monuments of Scotland.* H.M.S.O., 2nd. edn. 1964.

DILLON, M. & CHADWICK, N. K. *The Celtic realms* Weidenfeld & Nicolson, 1967. reprinting no date.

HANSON, R. P. C. & BARLEY, M. W. *Christianity in Britain, 300–700* Leicester U.P., 1968.

HENDERSON, I. *The Picts* Thames & Hudson, 1967. op.

MACQUEEN, J. *St Nynia: a study of literary and linguistic evidence* Oliver & Boyd, 1961.

THOMAS, C. *The early Christian archaeology of North Britain* O.U.P., 1971.

WAINWRIGHT, F. T. ed. *The problem of the Picts* Nelson, 1955. op.

WATSON, W. J. *History of the Celtic place-names of Scotland* Blackwood, 1926. op.

Chapter 8

BROGGER, A. W. *Ancient emigrants* O.U.P., 1929. op.

HAMILTON, J. R. C. *Excavations at Jarlshof, Shetland* H.M.S.O., 1956. op.

SHETELIG, H. *Viking antiquities in Great Britain and Ireland, vols. I. & II.* Oslo, Aschehoug, 1940. op.

WAINWRIGHT, F. T. ed. *The northern isles* Nelson, 1962. op.

Chapters 9 and 10

BARROW, G. W. S. *Feudal Britain* Ed. Arnold, 1956.

BARROW, G. W. S. *Robert Bruce and the community of the Realm of Scotland* Eyre & Spottiswoode, 1965. op.

DICKINSON, W. C. *Scotland from the earliest times to 1603* Nelson, 1961.

DICKINSON, W. C. ed. *Early records of the Burgh of Aberdeen* Constable, 1957. op.

POWICKE, Sir M. *The thirteenth century, 1216–1307* O.U.P., 2nd. edn. 1962.

RENN, D. F. *Norman castles in Britain* J. Baker, 1968.

RITCHIE, R. L. G. *The Normans in Scotland* Edinburgh University P., 1954. op.

Index